O. Jefferson

Report of the semi-centennial and seventy-fifth anniversaries of the settlement of Wayne Township, Ashtabula County, Ohio

August 24th, 1853 and 1878

O. Jefferson

Report of the semi-centennial and seventy-fifth anniversaries of the settlement of Wayne Township, Ashtabula County, Ohio
August 24th, 1853 and 1878

ISBN/EAN: 9783743328051

Manufactured in Europe, USA, Canada, Australia, Japa

Cover: Foto ©ninafisch / pixelio.de

Manufactured and distributed by brebook publishing software (www.brebook.com)

O. Jefferson

Report of the semi-centennial and seventy-fifth anniversaries of the settlement of Wayne Township, Ashtabula County, Ohio

REPORT

OF THE

SEMI-CENTENNIAL

AND

Seventy-Fifth Anniversaries

OF THE

SETTLEMENT

OF

WAYNE TOWNSHIP,

ASHTABULA COUNTY, OHIO.

AUGUST 24TH, 1853 AND 1878.

JEFFERSON, O.:
PRINTED BY D. LEE & SON.
1879.

PRELIMINARY PROCEEDINGS.

At a meeting of the citizens of Wayne, held on the 2nd day of November, A. D., 1852, being the day of Presidential Election, it was

RESOLVED, That we celebrate the Semi-Centennial Anniversary of the settlement of Wayne Township, during the coming year, and that all persons who have formerly resided in our Township, be respectfully invited to meet with us.

RESOLVED, That Williamsfield, which once constituted a portion of the Township, be included, and that its inhabitants be cordially invited to join with us in celebrating said Anniversary.

RESOLVED, That a Committee of five be duly appointed, who shall have full power to name the day and make the needful preparation.

Whereupon the following named persons were appointed:—
CALVIN C. WICK, JOSHUA FOBES, Jr., HIRAM A. BABCOCK, RICHARD HAYES and SYLVESTER WARD.

The Committee were instructed to designate the day for a gathering of the citizens, and to give due notice of the same. It was sincerely hoped and trusted that the occasion would be so interesting as fully to compensate any and all of our former citizens, as well as present residents, for attending. Adjourned.

C. C. WICK, Secretary.

HIRAM A. BABCOCK, Chairman.
WAYNE, November 2nd, 1852.

Notice was duly given to the Trustees, and some of the principal citizens of Williamsfield, of the above named invitation.

The Committee were notified to meet at the Counting Room of C. C. Wick, on the 24th of March, 1853, at 1 o'clock, P. M.

C. C. WICK, Chairman.

March 24th, 1853.—Committee met, agreeably to appointment, and made the following arrangements:—

The celebration will take place on the 24th day of August, 1853. The following Officers and Committees were appointed:

President .... CALVIN C. WICK.
Vice Presidents .... LINUS H. JONES, J. B. BARBER, J. FOBES, Jr.
Secretaries .... ORCUTT R. WARD, CHARLES FITCH.
Treasurer .... JOSHUA FOBES, Jr.
Marshals .... RICHARD HAYES, NOAH BARTHOLOMEW.
Assistant Marshals .... WM. C. WICK, LORENZO D. GILLETT, ELON HART, HORACE F. GIDDINGS, CHESTER OATMAN, ALBERT HAYES, LUCIUS GILLETT, SAMUEL JONES, Jr., DAVID HART, JAMES W. KENEDY.
Chaplain .... HIRAM A. BABCOCK.
Speakers .... Hon. JOSHUA R. GIDDINGS, Rev. E. B. CHAMBERLAIN, Rev. DANIEL H. BABCOCK.
Com. on Entertainment.. SYLVESTER WARD, J. FOBES, JR., ANSON JONES, L. H. JONES, DAVID PARKER, N. COLEMAN, Jr., HORACE F. GIDDINGS, MORRIS SPELLMAN, LEVI J. FOBES.
Com. to prepare a place of meeting .... } H. A. BABCOCK, JAMES LILLIE, S. JONES, Jr., RICHARD HAYES, BENONI ANDREWS, S. WARD, L. H. JONES, WM. COLEMAN.
Com. on Finance .... J. FOBES, Jr., J. B. BARBER, N. COLEMAN, Jr., HORACE GIDDINGS, SIMON P. FOBES, LEVI J. FOBES, ANSON JONES, MORRIS SPELLMAN.
Com. on Police and Order of the day .... } CALVIN C. WICK, ANSON JONES, RICHARD HAYES, NOAH BARTHOLOMEW, ALBERT HAYES, D. HART.
Com. on Music .... LINUS H. JONES, G. C. HOLT, O. R. WARD.

ELISHA GIDDINGS was duly appointed a leader of the Ancient Choir, and to collect a suitable number to form a Choir, and that the Church Choir and Glee Club be invited to attend.

C. C. WICK, Chairman.

O. R. WARD,
C. FITCH, } Secretaries.

The Anniversary.

The first half-century celebration of the settlement of the Township of Wayne, was held at that place on the 24th day of August, 1853, and attended by a large number of the citizens of the Township and County.

Quite a spirit of excitement had exhibited itself for some time previous, particularly among "the old folks" of our usually quiet place, consequent on the celebration, for the first time, of the anniversary of the day when the first settlers of our Township founded a home among its unbroken forests.

Early on the morning of the anniversary the rain commenced falling, and continued till a late hour in the forenoon, which rendered it impossible to proceed to the Grove as intended, when it was determined to resort to the Center Church, which, in a short time, was densely filled.

After a call to order by the President, the exercises of the day were commenced by singing by the Choir, (consisting of JOHN S. FITCH, Conductor, Mr. HOLT, organist, and Linus H. Jones, Anson Giddings, Azel B. Fobes, Melancthon Andrews, Charles Fitch, Chancey Fitch, Chester Fitch, Mrs. Chamberlain, Mrs. Anson Giddings, Mrs. Ely, Miss Flora Krum, Miss Lucy Parker, Miss Lucy Daniels, Miss Cornelia Roe, Miss Harriet Hayes, Miss May C. Miner,) the following lines :—

>Joyful, joyful, joyful be our numbers,
>Bursting forth the soul-enliv'ning lay;
>Swell the strain to music's sweetest murmurs,
>Every heart now hail the festal day.
>>Hail, O hail, this festal day.
>From the hill and valley far away,
>We come with merry greetings in our lay.
>Yearly as our festal day rolls round,
>We hail it ever with harmonious sound.

The Rev. G. ROBERTS, Pastor of the Church in West Williamsfield, then read from a very ancient Bible,* which once belonged to the great-grandmother of the first settlers of the township, the following selected portions of scripture:—

"Remember the days of old, consider the years of many generations. Ask thy Father and he will show thee; thy elders, and they will tell thee. When the Most High divided to the nations their inheritance, when he separated the sons of Adam, he set the borders of the people according to the number of the children of Israel. For the Lord's portion is his people; Jacob is the lot of his inheritance. He found him in a desert land, and in the waste howling wilderness; he led him about, he instructed him, he kept him as the apple of his eye. As an eagle stirreth up her nest, fluttereth over her young, spreadeth abroad her wings, taketh them, beareth them on her wings; so the Lord alone did lead him, and there was no strange god with him. He made him ride on the high places of the earth, that he might eat the increase of the fields; and he made him to suck honey out of the rock, and oil out of the flinty rock; butter of kine, and milk of sheep, with fat of lambs, and rams of the breed of Bashan, and goats, with the fat of kidneys of wheat; and thou didst drink the pure blood of the grape. (Deut. 32: 7-15.) Then shalt thou cause the trumpet of the jubilee to sound. * * * And ye shall hallow the fiftieth year, and proclaim liberty throughout all the land unto all the inhabitants thereof: it shall be a jubilee unto you; and ye shall return every man unto his possession, and ye shall return every man unto his family. A jubilee shall the fiftieth year be unto you: * * * It shall be holy unto you: and ye shall return every man unto his own possession. (Lev. 25: 9-13.) Ye shall dwell in booths seven days: all that are Israelites born shall dwell in booths: That your generations may know that I made the children of Israel to dwell in booths, when I brought them out of the land of Egypt: I am the LORD your God. (Lev. 23: 42, 43.) If ye shall hearken dilligently unto my commandments which I command you this day, to love the LORD your God, and to serve him with all your heart and with all your soul, I will give *you* the rain of your land in his due season, the first rain and the latter rain, that thou mayest gather in thy corn, and thy wine, and thine oil. And I will send grass in thy fields for thy cattle, that thou mayest eat and be full. (Deut. 11: 13-15.)"

An appropriate prayer was offered by HIRAM A. BABCOCK. The Choir then sung the following original hymn, written for the Anniversary of the settlement of Wayne, by the Rev. D. H. BABCOCK:

I.

Forests have gone, wild beasts have fled;
Around us lie the pious dead
 Of fifty changing years.
We meet to speak of days of yore,
Of deeds and men now gone before,
 With blended smiles and tears.

---

*This Bible once belonged to Abigail Fobes. Her son, Captain Simon Fobes, and Thankful, his wife, moved to Wayne, in November, 1807, and died the following February, having lived together more than fifty years, and being separated only three days in death. Their graves, and those of their sons, Simon and Nathan, with their wives, and also the grave of one of their daughters, may be seen, side by side in the Center burying ground. All having lived to a very advanced age, averaging more than eighty years.

II.

And first to God our notes we'll raise;
For all the past we offer praise,
   And for the future pray;—
Then round the founders of this place,
A worthy and a godly race,
   Our memories shall fling.

III.

Then all who've taught in sacred things,
Or given to science golden wings
   On which aloft to soar,
Shall be remembered at this hour,
For now we feel their genial power,
   And hope to evermore.

IV.

We'll call to mind each honored name,
Who held a place of trust or fame
   In this our happy town;
Their days of toil have not been lost,
Whate'er the skill, whate'er the cost,
   They've given to her renown.

V.

Those by whose toil the fields now bloom,
Or by the workshop or the loom
   Her comforts have supplied;
To skilled physicians, merchantmen
And statesmen of the deepest ken,
   Our hearts we open wide.

VI.

Ye townsmen come, ye friends draw near,
And strangers, too, you're welcome here
   On this inspiring day—
Day which to us ne'er came before,
And will revisit us no more
   While here on earth we stay.

The President then remarked as follows:—

FRIENDS AND FELLOW CITIZENS:—An interesting and pleasing duty is assigned to me, to tender to this assembly and these invited guests a salutation of welcome to the Semi-Centennial Anniversary of this Township.

We meet not to commemorate deeds of blood, nor to carry out a partizan project, but to commemorate an important event in our history, and to do honor to our venerable ancestors who are alive, and render proper respect to the memory of those who are dead. But, Friends, we welcome you to our rural shades, and sincerely trust you will enjoy the festivities of this Anniversary. We seek not to gratify any selfish ambition, nor to attract the eye, but to render an honest welcome to our venerable parents and invited guests.

An interesting duty now devolves upon me, to call together our venerable Fathers and Mothers, and especially the first Pioneers, which is truly an interesting and impressive sight.

I now introduce to you the first of the band, JOSHUA FOBES, and DOLLY FOBES, his wife. They came to this township in 1803, and have "borne the burden and heat of the day." I thank God they live to commemorate this day. And, my dear sir, in behalf of this vast assembly, I tender you our congratulations and best wishes, for yourself and lady.

We would now introduce to you ELISHA GIDDINGS, and PHILOTHETA, his wife. They came to this township in 1805, two years after Mr. FOBES. We are glad that Uncle Elisha and good kindhearted Aunt Phila are permitted to live to celebrate this day.

We would introduce to you Mrs. PHEBE HAYES, widow of TITUS HAYES, *deceased*. They came to the township at the same time Mr. GIDDINGS came; they settled near each other and shared each other's joys and sorrows. While Mr. GIDDINGS is permitted to enjoy the honors of this day, his pioneer companion lies in "yonder grave yard." How many hearts in this assembly will swell with emotion and affection at the name of TITUS HAYES! He still lives in the memory of all who knew him, and we can but tender to his widow our sympathies, and render *her* the honors. What is her loss is ours. May we strive to emulate his virtues.

All attention seemed drawn to that portion of the audience which occupied the seats around the pulpit. There sat the "Pioneers" —noble men and women "of other days;" and during the forenoon the venerable forms of the early settlers of our Township and County might be seen pressing their way through the densely crowded aisles to join that noble band who had met "to speak of days and deeds of yore."

Directly in front of the pulpit sat the Ancient Choir, under the leadership of that veteran "son of song," Uncle ELISHA GIDDINGS,

With his soul full of music, and his heart full of cheer.

The names of the members who composed the Ancient Choir

were: Elisha Giddings (chorister) and wife, Joshua Fobes and wife, Simon Fobes and wife, Charles Walworth and wife, Joel Blakeslee, John Woodworth, Rebecca Andrews, Samuel L. Holcomb, Mrs. Hori Miner, Joshua Giddings, Mr. Beman, Luther Spellman, Reuben Russell, Loton Fobes and wife Dolly, and Captain Justus Fobes.

The exercises were now enlivened by a "toot" from the good old fashioned "pitch pipe," which gave the key in good old fashioned style, to the tune of "Whitestown,"in which was sung the following stanzas:

> "Where nothing dwelt but beasts of prey,
> And men as fierce and wild as they,
> He bids th' opprest and poor repair,
> And builds them towns and cities there.
>
> "They sow the fields, and trees they plant,
> Whose yearly fruit supplies their wants;
> Their race grows up from fruitful stock,
> Their wealth increases with their flocks,"

Selected from the Puritanic Psalm, commencing

> "When God, provok'd with daring crimes."

The following Poem, written for the occasion, was then presented to the audience:

POEM.

BY REV. E. B. CHAMBERLAIN.

> Half centuries are the small dots
>   On time's broad dial-plate;
> Way-marks set up to show the world
>   How early or how late.
> As patriarchs raise a stone of help,
>   Or statesmen build a tower—
> Lest mercies past should be forgot
>   In age's oblivious power—
>
> So we are summoned here to-day,
>   A numerous, thoughtful throng,
> To raise a mile-stone at the close
>   Of fifty twelve-months long.
> Strange thoughts are flocking in our minds;
>   Thoughts hitherto concealed.
> A hidden fountain in our hearts
>   We feel is now unsealed.

Full fifty times the frigid cloak
  Of winter, fall did bring;
And fifty times the robin birds
  Have caroled in the spring;
And fifty times the velvet leaves
  Of forest trees appeared;
And fifty times the autumn frosts
  Their plumage gay hath seared;

And fifty times the snowy tribes
  Of merry skipping lambs
Have frolicked for the gay pastime
  Of proud and fleecy dams;
Twice fifty times triangle flocks,
  With songs of emigration,
From north to south, and south to north,
  Have leagued their wonted station.

And five times ten most aptly mark
  The mile-stones of the free;
For God hath measured by such time
  The ancient jubilee.
But if we lacked a precedent
  In times remote or near,
The noon of nineteenth century
  Would make its fitness clear.

Since days and years commenced their course,
  Or earth began to be,
What change and progress have been wrought
  Enlivening land and sea.
But proudest dreams of ancient sage
  In loftiest fancy caught
When visions in soft reveries
  By silent starlight brought,

With us are more than hope and wish
  And mind's exhilaration;
Realities more strange to us
  Than their imagination,
Unfolding Heaven's exalted plan,
  As chalked by prophet's pen—
By swift-winged angels o'er the earth
  To bring good news to men.

Your needful task is self-imposed—
  Review eventful *time*.
What has been done since these rich fields
  Were in their forest prime?
Time *past* and *future* we may grant;
  But *present* time's a fiction,
'Twas ne'er allowed, or e'er can be
  By any proper diction.

Unless when sun and moon stood still
  At Joshua's bold command;
Or when at last time stops its course
  By that uplifted hand
Of angel in Apocalypse,
  With one foot on the sea
And one on land to execute
  The will of Deity.

No—we own time as men own streams
  Running in channeled courses;
In motion useful—but at rest,
  Like Phætons without horses.
Then grieve not of time's rapid flight,
  It brought it's faithful dower.
Ring out this day your jubilee
  As clocks strike out the hour.

" Who led thee through that wilderness
  So terrible and great?"*
Said God to Joshua, past the snares
  Of danger's dreadful seat.
What led thee father Joshua Fobes,
  In eighteen hundred three
To leave fair Tolland and the State
  That borders on the sea?

For unshorn plains and trackless wilds,
  If you the cost had counted
Would you have ventured on the task
  And every ill surmounted?
Your " better half" has well remarked—
  " What needs this endless sorrow?
For care came fast enough for me—
  I did not wish to borrow!"

Well might she trust—for twelfth of June
  Gave papers of insurance
That you would stand 'twixt her and harm
  For mortal life's endurance.
JOSHUA—a household word with her—
  Almost a mellow tripthong—
And her good name now sounds with yours
  Like vowels in a dipthong.

You took your land, as some folks say
  Fond husbands take their wives—
" Unsight--unseen," "for best or worst,"
  And 'bide it all their lives.
Range number two, town number eight,
  Summed up your whole inspection.
But promised land—Western Reserve—
  Was safe with such selection.

---

*Deut. 8; 15.

Romance becomes reality,
  With calls of wandering savage—
And bears and wolves alternately
  Lay wait your home to ravage;
Sickness comes on—"do let us go
  Enjoy a brighter sky."
"No," says your help-meet, "here's my home
  And here I'll live or die!"

Among the *luxuries* of home
  In "twelve by fourteen" cabins
Were stone-back chimneys, puncheon floors,
  And—proud as Jewish Rabbins—
Were men, when moved so far "up town"
  That they were truly able
To say *our bedsteads, chairs* and *door*,
  Our pantry and our table.

Each man kept open cabin then
  With latch-string out of door;
And lodged as many welcomed guests
  As trode the sand-white floor.
That same old arm-chair that you see
  Arrayed upon the stand
Has held Gid, Granger and a host
  Of worthies in the land—

Of doctors, lawyers, clergymen,
  And royal yoemen, charged
With true nobility, that you
  Well-name "Yankees enlarged."
The *chair's* the same—I care not now
  How often 'twas new seated—
As we keep our identity
  By mending oft repeated.

'Twas quite a pardonable cheat
  To hold the hopeful West
As *few* men keep a garrison,
  And show their force at best.
To make the tale of households large,
  As truth might seem to be.
You counted then two bachelors
  To make one family.

The *principles* you planted here
  Challenge the world's inspection'
And from their purity we hope
  There is no sad defection.
Justice and *freedom* you have taught
  Were no mere loose abstractions,
And watch the laws with jealous care
  To save them from infractions.

The fundamental elements
  That make a statute *legal*
Were sought for, not in enactments
  Republican or regal.
That cannot be monopolized
  Which God has made for each,
Nor sun, nor air, nor truth, self-shown
  Beyond a question's reach.

Law hath its limits—wide indeed
  The range it may pass—through
All things humane, and all things just,
  All interests old and new;
But there are lines as fixed as fate,
  That if this legal courser
Transcends, (this truth's of ancient date,)
  He's but a vile *usurper*.

Blackstone himself would just as soon
  Have hoped to build a mansion,
By laying the foundation stones
  On ether up towards Heaven,
As to construct by wholesome rules
  A tower of jurisprudence,
On any pillars less than these:
  God and the rights of conscience.

Laws may be *weak, at fault, unjust*,
  And sorely we may feel them;
Still we are bound to own their sway
  Until we can repeal them.
But cross the truth that God exists,
  Or man's right to be free,
All semblance of a law is lost
  In unmixed tyranny.

Guard well this truth (tho' ne'er an age
  That has produced a faction,
With pusillanimous pretence
  Of conscience-bound exaction,
With *morbid* conscience, warped and weak;
  And—if you'll take their word—
Are "heaven's elected" malcontents,
  And cut-throats " in the Lord,")

You're all at sea, on floating isles,
  With no fixed habitation,
Unless you grant that man has rights
  Above all legislation.
Man cannot make the *substratum*
  On which all *law* is built,
Nor ever trample on the same
  Without most damning guilt.

This truth, the winds and waking breath
   Of every morning breeze,
With every evening zephyr's voice,
   That sighs among these trees,
Has taught you all, with Blackstone's notes
   And Paley's explanation,
With sacred scripture—surest guide—
   In all such litigation.

They called you "breakers of the *law*,"
   Because with righteous scorn
You disobeyed that "Compromise,"
   A measure most forlorn.
Give you a murderer for a friend!
   A demon for a brother!
Serpents for fish—to trusting babes
   From hands of sire and mother!

'Twere bad enough, and quite too hard
   To see *o'erboard* a child;
But when he'd summond all his strength,
   And in his terror wild
Had reached the boat and clenched his hold,
   To be compelled to stand
With ax upraised and coolly cut
   The faint boy's feeble hand—

Were equal only to the task
   Of sending back the *free*,
Who pant to save the priceless boon
   Of sacred liberty.
If you've a townsman that would help
   To bind the hateful chain
On limbs of innocense and grief
   To toil in bonds again,

With sorrowing heart youd' bid him go
   To dark Bedouin tribes
Of treacherous Arabs in the East,
   And serve *them* for their bribes.
Go, if you must—darken the door
   Of the wild Hottentot;
But o'er our rose-bound cottage lawn
   Your swarthy shade cast not.

If statutes sin against yourself
   Your loyalty is good,
Tho' you submit to all their claim
   And yield your wealth and blood;
But when they claim that you shall wrong
   Your *neighbor* or your *God*,
You're only loyal when you scorn
   Both Statute and its rod.

Some rocks hem in ambitious seas
   Rebuking maddened waves ;
Some truths fence in all *legal* pranks
   For freemen or for slaves ;
Tread utmost verge to maintain *law*,
   And prize protection, too,
But "If foundations be destroyed
   What can the righteous do ?"

Your moral code is Puritan,
   For this we may be grateful.
The history of your settlement
   Records no crime that's hateful.
If principles by May-Flower brought
   Should surname you as " blue ;"
The cognomen, tho' out of taste,
   You cheerful own as true.

Those things in nature we admire
   Are not much given to change,
Whether we gaze at heaven's broad arch
   Or on the ocean range.
The sky is so " conservative,"
   It never changed its hue ;
Tenacious as a Puritan
   It holds its ancient blue.

The deep wide sea with steadfast course,
   Tho' much " behind the time,"
Is blue to-day as when of old
   'Twas colored in its prime ;
Is *blue* diminutively used
   To mark a moral spleen?
We note, things fickle, crude and raw
   Are sometimes labeled "green."

How can you show the beautiful
   In change and healthful progress,
Unless you have a staid ground work
   Unchanging on your canvas !
Key notes in music love *new* sounds,
   And ne'er despise their youth ;
So Puritans welcome *new views*,
   Unless they " jar" with truth.

Creation's work must be undone,
   Redemption be unwrought,
Before the Sabbath's sacred hours
   To uselessness are brought ;
And Holy Scripture second best—
   Fancy, foremost unfurled,
When children bring their parents up,
   And give them to the world.

A licensed dram-shop never stained
  The five-miles-square of Wayne;
Nor ever "*mania a potu*"
  A single victim slain.
This was foreshown by Joshua's wife,
  To Massassauger Tribe,
Who could not then foretell this fact
  As well as history's scribe!

The Indians often came for drink,
  And what must Joshua do?
They took the glass, wishing good health
  With their "Tunamacoo."
The glass returned, they are good friends
  As Savages may be.
And bowing thankfully they mouth
  Their wonted " *Wa-wa-ne.*"

They once *demand* this beverage
  Of Dorothy his wife,
And threatening with angry tones
  They raised the scalping knife;
But woman's might was woman's right—
  In absence of her groom
She fought a half-score of this tribe,
  And drove them *with her broom.*

Tho' now your population's great
  And wealth a bounteous store,
We search in vain from house to house
  To find a drunkard's door.
The facts prove you temperance vanguard,
  And if the Law of Maine
Is sought in County or in State
  You've pledged the vote of Wayne.

That stone house at the Capitol
  You've never patronized:
Its grates and bars and sombre halls
  Perhaps you have not prized;
A gloomy penitentiary
  You judged was not in taste,
For children of your Dorothy,
  And none have been disgraced.

You've reared for honorable trade
  A quantum sent to college,
And furnish good facilities
  For academic knowledge.
You have, 'tis true, some quite *fast* youth
  Who walk behind cigars,
Like baby-locomotive steeds
  When puffing in the cars.

They walk with crooked headed canes
   And sport their silver watches,
And comb their beards and dress their manes
   And nourish their mustaches;
They smack their wine and thread their "yarns,"
   While each the oath endorses—
Fast boys, fast men, fast beards, fast oaths,
   Fast bargains and fast horses.

There's consolation, tho' we see
   A figure minus signed
By horizontal dash prefixed,
   Its *total's* not resigned—
By something it is thence made less;
   But still it may be used,
So prefix smoke stems, only show
   Young wise heads *some* reduced.

The favored age we chronicle
   Is starred with brighter gems
Then ever were bestowed on earth
   In age's diadems.
The power of steam by Fulton's art,
   If dates are rightly given,
Was tested on the stream with boat
   In eighteen hundred seven.

The piston rod in pressing steam,
   To gain a locomotion,
Was long decried as offspring of
   A visionary notion.
To-day this power is harnessed down
   To draw o'er every sea
The wealth of nations and the pride
   Of art and industry.

And fiery, snorting, iron steeds,
   Over our public ways,
Have changed fatigue and care to ease,
   And moments into days.
Those ancient music instruments
   Are fading out of fashion,
For which our mothers entertained
   So great a love and passion.

Accordeon *cards*, melodeon *wheels*,
   And parlor organ *looms*—
If some choice relics still survive
   They're found in attic rooms.
This power is turning all machines
   Not trundled by a stream,
And printing by the gross, forsooth,
   Is done by "Fulton's dream."

We've seen a fiercer agent tamed,
  With marvel interest heightening,
Collared and "broke," and way-wise taught,
  The headstrong fraction's lightning.
Franklin, 'tis true, with matchless skill
  Made a successful throw,
And caught the ranger in the snare
  Of his improved lasso.

But 'twas reserved for this age
  That our Professor Morse
Should show the practicable use
  Of this subdued mail horse.
We open trade and close contracts
  With eastern city traders,
And talk with western editors
  Of danger and invaders.

We speak, our friends five hundred miles
  In sickness, death and sorrow,
And they are with us, at our side
  By afternoon to-morrow.
These wondrous wires like feeling nerves
  That tell of ease and pain,
Quick as electric shock report
  The case up to the brain.

If danger seize our Government
  In the extremest part
Of this great "body politic,"
  It's felt too at the heart.
So much at least is this the fact,
  By use of magnet poles,
The gray adage is absolete,
  That "nations have no souls."

But the peculiar happy charm
  That burnished every page
Of the half century we embalm,
  Most *philanthropic* age—
The blind, the dumb, the lunatic,
  Of reason quite run wild—
The helpless widow bowed with grief,
  And Sighing orphan child

Have State asylums all humane,
  Built as by mercy's hands
With voluntary christian care,
  Rather than State demands,
Which mostly take their root and growth
  Within these fifty years,
As if a succoring Heaven was moved
  By sorrow's ceaseless tears.

That Missionary Board was formed
  In eighteen hundred ten,
Which takes the name "American,"
  To reach all tribes of men.
Our stations now star continents,
  And islands of the sea;
A yearly quarter million paid
  One tithe of charity.

In eighteen hundred and sixteen
  'Twas judged the time had come
To give all men the Sacred Word
  Despite the see of Rome.
The Bible to all men on earth,
  With a complete translation,
For freedom's guardian star of hope,
  And personal salvation.

In fifty dialects, twice told,
  Retrenching power of lungs,
You preach a Savior crucified
  By modern gift of tongues.
There is no age since time began
  That wears upon its brow
Such gilded glory as that age
  We're contemplating now,

Excepting always the glad day
  When came the Prince of Peace—
Fair Bethlehem's star—the world's sole hope—
  From darkness to release.
Who would have lived in earlier times
  When action was restrained?
Or who would live in later years
  When the world's conquest's gained?

If rest is sweetend by our toil—
  If soldiers prize their freedom—
Was joy before Messiah set,
  In garments dyed from Edom?
With inward praise let us rejoice
  That Heaven assigned *our* day
In times of toil, and hope, and gain,
  Of freedom's glorious sway.

Your town named for "Mad Anthony,"
  Alias General Wayne,
At Monmouth field or Stony Point
  Was sure the day to win.
'Twas something of a venture made
  To nail your flag so high
As bold and fearless Ajax WAYNE,
  Yet prudent Anthony.

Farmed out by lines in perfect square,
  With interest so much blended,
If you had feuds or party strifes
  They long ere this have ended.
"Lands intersect by narrow friths"
  Would fain "abhor each other;
So Pymatuning's frothy stream
  Drove brother from his brother,

Leaving your parish minus some
  Whose worth is not concealed,
With bodies in the town of Wayne,
  And souls in Williamsfield.
A monstrous torture some might think—
  A strange and sad divorcement—
But elective affinity
  Serves better than enforcement.

A sickly-headed simpleton
  Once gravely laid it down
That this would one day surely be
  A famous *seaport* town;
But while you gaily point your wits
  Of inland on the sea,
The world that goes by "starts and fits"
  Conceals your destiny.

It has a way with rails and steam,
  And wires and conjugation,
To place you near to any point
  Within the land or nation.
That fools and children speak the truth
  Is not so much a notion,
Since now *perhaps* the Air Line Road
  Will move you to the ocean.

Of men revered as magistrates,
  Starting from early days,
With honor resting on his head,
  We name Judge Titus Hayes—
In judgment, just—an upright man—
  A pattern for his station,
And, like the *road* that bears his name,
  Was free from deviation.

Twenty-one years, last second month,
  You bore him to his grave,
And every time your feet have pressed
  The grounds his bounty gave,
With the pale dust of sheeted dead
  Who've closed their earthly race—
Pathetic thought—their final home,
  Deeded by Titus Hayes.

With justice Flavel, there has gone
   Lamented Drayton Jones,
With the craped list you've treasured up
   Of your departed ones.
That magistrate who longest served,
   Elected by your *poll-men*,
To hold the scales of justice even,
   Was Esq. Nathaniel Coleman.

Thirty-one years, excess by ten,
   Of his minority,
Obeying the potential call
   Of Wayne's majority.
And many more whose worth perhaps
   'Tis best we leave unsaid,
Till time's proud march shall write them too
   As numbered with the dead.

There is a class revered and loved,
   Who with you bear a part,
Whose calling is by most men named
   The *cure* or *healing art*.
You curse them days and seek them nights—
   (How health and sickness differ)
Locusts of Egypt—Angel guests,
   What loggerheads are stiffer?

By blazed-tree paths, through fenceless wilds,
   Did Doctor Allen come,
With faithful care, at your request,
   Sought your afflicted home.
And—Æsculapius! what a tribe
   Are sometimes "called" to ride
For "love of God," and "charity,"
   And something more beside.

But of good lancets, one had rights
   Excelling all the rest;
Both friend and foe acknowledged this,
   And called him Doctor *Best*.
For if *divine rights* are allowed
   To kings and their succession,
Practitioners must "stand for rights"
   Of patronymic blessing.

On Pymatuning's sunrise side
   There long lived one physician,
Who, for a safe and quiet ride,
   Enjoyed a good position.
He gave the fevers such a *spell*
   That every sick and well man,
By universal, just consent,
   Pronounced him Doctor *Spelman*.

That Doctor, now, who guides the plough
  In the south-eastern valley,
And leaves his folio with his peers
  Upon their wits to rally,
Thinks, much with us to make a fuss
  With an o'er-loaded thorax,
Is labor lost beside the cost
  Of mercury and borax.

But he who judges him at fault
  In ken and self-reliance,
Had better measure lines with him
  In fathoming this science.
Amidst a hundred graduates,
  Contented with their tickets,
He tortured Nature on the rack,
  And made her tell some secrets.

He holds that in the world's best days,
  As shown in sacred books,
That swords to ploughshares must be beat,
  And spears to pruning-hooks.
But still, if there are broken bones,
  Or sickness comes that's stallworth,
The people make it quite a point
  To call on Doctor *Walworth*.

Of neighbors near 'tis hard to speak,
  Except with mouth quite mealy,
But, if in taste, we'd speak one word
  Commending Doctor Ely.
There still is one beyond my reach,
  Full-grown Apollo's son,
And when you need a counselor,
  You turn to Hamilton.

There's one, alas, we all lament,
  May heaven grant that we,
Like Luther Loomis Woodworth, die
  Without an enemy.
If you will take our free advice
  Of these detested drugs,
Wait till you're sick before you call
  The Doctors all humbugs.

By *families* may we review
  At risk of some omission,
'Twer better that your names were called
  By one of your commission.
Most of you show your *major* state
  By years and life's refiners,
But there are some, in spite of age,
  Who always will be *Miners*.

Allied to these by some near ties,
  A hive that has no drones,
A family with one side Hayes,
  The house of *Samuel Jones;*
With *Samuel Junior*, and a *Esq.*,
  And music no way minus
Since on their record we may read
  Of such a name as *Linus.*

A race of Fobes, *thrice Simon* pure,
  Corruption could not bribe.
Branching you find our *Joshua*,
  And then fair Levi's tribe.
Elias, too, at twelve years old
  Sought here his forest home,
When these fair plains were pathless woods
  For savage beasts to roam,

The house of Benjamin, 'tis thought,
  Were given you for guards,
For he who looks your history through
  Will see the town has *Wards.*
One of this name became extinct,
  But not as life gives o'er;
If not securely in an ark,
  Is quite bound up in *Noah.*

Another, blended with a *Wick*,
  A strange yet pleasing sight,
Went out, as doth a morning star,
  And lost herself in light.
Guarded with sentinels most true
  And of experience long,
" Race is not always to the swift
  Or battle to the strong,"

But if a pin or screw was loose
  On either side the wheel,
The Wards were always at their post,
  The fractured place to heal.
Whether 'twas township, church or school,
  An easter or a wester,
There's nothing ever yet escaped
  The notice of *Sylvester*.

The ancient house of Nathan Fobes
  Is here well represented,
Equal inheritors, I'm sure
  It's nothing we've invented.
Disyllabled is every name :
  Jabez, David, Oshea,
Justus and Loton all in town,
  With Nathan industry ;

We shall not give you half your due,
  Make one hair black or white;
More stings than honey you may get,
  Or wrong instead of right.
Since Elon means a grove of oaks,
  And David slew a giant,
There's reason why one Parker's bold,
  And one more mildly pliant.

Good dignitaries you might have
  For churchmen's diocese,
Since there are Deans who sit for life
  To show your *footsteps* peace.
Then Scripture names for *Bartons* given
  Both Eldad and Eli,
And Giddings, more than I dare name,
  Or could, if I should try.

But one to serve for specimen,
  As brick to show the building,
I point to "Uncle Elisha" here,
  Whose history needs no guilding;
The leader of this Ancient Choir,
  As you to-day have seen,
Teaching us how the gammut rolled
  When they were but eighteen.

One we *should* name, more widely known
  By his conspicuous station,
At Washington for fifteen years
  In councils of the nation.
Our people would not interfere
  With slave laws in the States,
But held that sovereignties must judge
  What best to them relates.

But when the bold presumptious step
  Was taken in our sight
Rudely to wed *us* with the curse,
  Perforce, with "main and might"—
Yes, when the *body of this death*
  Upon our backs was forced,
You vowed by all your heaven-born rights,
  The curse should be divorced.

The people sought to speak their minds,
  No fearful dodging mute,
But head to think, and heart to feel,
  And hand to execute.
How well they judged 'tis not for us
  To say, or what he's done;
For Wayne will leave the world to tell
  The firmness of his son.

One truth became a chronic fact,
　Unless the "record blunders,"
He "stood" the scorching southern fires
　As Teneriffe breaks thunders.
Aspersion called him "fool-hardy,"
　The "one-idea" member,
For slavery burdened every theme,
　From first month to December.

Cato, of Roman Senate, laid
　On Carthage an embargo,
And ended every forum speech
　" Delenda est Carthago!"
Your kinsman struck at every point,
　The "wrong," the "shame," the "knavery"
Of freeman forced into support
　Of cruel chattel slavery.

When once the slave-power sent him home,
　With papers and commission,
Unanimous the people said
　'Twas not a *fair* dismission.
With indignation rather tart,
　Abating party strife,
We sent him back to serve his term,
　And some have said for life.

And this we did, not quite so much
　Because we loved our Reed,
As that our manly self-respect
　Was outraged by the deed.
'Twas not for Cæsar but for Rome,
　The brave Italians fought,
'Twas not your townsman, but the rights
　Of freemen, that we sought.

Attached to him! indeed—but lay
　The weight of his small finger
On freedom's cause, to check its growth,
　Would retribution linger?
You'd blot his name from out your books
　As Israel's scribes record
The sad apostasy of those
　Who have denied their Lord.

The fulcrum truths your townsman held,
　To give aggression battle;
Our North Free States *are not free soil*,
　To run down human cattle;
And one must show a better right
　To Euclid's sable brothers,
Than that his father once invoiced
　With cotton, their own mothers.

That we might just as well consent
   That *angels* should be sold,
As *man*, in God's own image made,
   Should be transferred for gold.
And when the name of slave is known
   Only in history,
Should these facts rise in prominence,
   'Twill be no mystery.

But this one truth is all we seek—
   Should now be here recorded:
He's one of you, and what he's done
   Will amply be rewarded.
And who succeeds, Hutchins or Jones,
   A Hitchcock or an Iddings,
Remember that from *Wayne* there sprung
   A man named J. Reed Giddings.

The faith is strictly orthodox,
   Of error a bold beacon.
Why should it not? the church so long
   Have *Calvin* for a deacon.
With office-holder by his side
   Of iron rectitude,
Go try your chaff on younger birds
   In hopes of "doing good."

And firmer yet, if heterodox
   Should ever plot a trick,
Well fortified in parson's son,
   By *Calvin Chapin Wick*.
A fabric firm, three-ply the make,
   If *naming* could ensure
A solid, safe and Christian house,
   For ages to endure.

Calvin's a fixture, noted fact!
   That no man yet has doubted,
And Chapin so long held his post
   At Rocky Hill, unrouted.
And if you need a household fair
   As city on a hill,
Your lamp, well trimmed with purest oil
   Full to its verge you fill.

Still, if you'd have a clear pure light,
   With no gray beams declining,
Near to the center of your oil
   You place a *Wick* clear shining.
Robins and Badger led the way,
   But the first settled preacher
Was Reverend Ephraim T. Woodruff,
   Your chosen scribe and teacher.

The patriarch pressed with the weight
  Of almost fourscore years,
Is here to-day, firm and erect,
  Far better than his fears.
You have his toils, and if his life
  Is lengthened yet a "span,"
"Rise up before the hoary head,
  And honor the old man."

That portion of the town that's given
  By fate to Master William,
Is safely trusted to the care
  Of one among the million;
For as he shows you "old landmarks"
  With compass and with chain,
He's better able to define
  Your moral loss and gain.

To *Father Latham* we must turn
  Your thoughts in tenderness;
And *Martin Wilcox*, both now gone,
  And from their labors rest.
And still there's *one* wakes lively thoughts
  As we his name record,
(No *man* should ever bear such name,)
  The *Reverend Francis Lord.*

We read that Silas Babcock came,
  In eighteen hundred eight,
Whose family justice forbids
  That we should underrate.
Three sons were college graduates,
  And men of sound reliance;
Four daughters, who seem much disposed
  To climb the hill of science.

There's no demand that we should name
  Their poets and their preachers,
Some of you have their well-wrought rhymes,
  And some claim them as teachers.
Old Plymouth claims one of the sons
  Which indicates the "stripe"
Of their theology and creed—
  Their views no doubt are "ripe."

One family of truest wealth
  We register as *rich:*
That is the noted, numerous house,
  Of *Deacon William Fitch.*
Eleven sons, all grown but one,
  Fostered in wisdom's ways,
Need give no bonds to bless the world
  In all succeeding days.

"Variety's the spice of life."
　To make your pathway milder,
Some men are *Lillys*, some are *Sweet*,
　Some, we admit, are *Wilder*:
Some are called *Oatmen*, others *Pease*,
　But if we're not mistaken,
Whatever else you may have saved,
　You're surely lost your *Bacon*.

Barbers and Wilcoxes. Harts and Platts,
　Fosters, Gilletts and Ball,—
But it is plain our space forbids
　That we should name you all.
If we the best reserve till last
　In making out your bill,
Then those who are not named at all,
　You may count *better still*.

'Twas not our wish to wire a song
　Of such a lengthy make,
But see your names disposed along
　Like raisins through a cake.
And if, through ignorance, we've left
　Some worthy deed unposted,
When once the table-cloth's removed,
　The actor will be toasted.

And "fifty years have passed away!"
　Are confident you're right?
All treasured up for one great day,
　To be brought forth to light.
Time is all safe; that can't be lost;
　Our chance of good may be,
But leger years will keep accounts
　To all eternity.

The ashy dead—and are they lost?
　Our Saviour had the grave
All well insured by his own death;
　It took them but to save.
Your influence—is that passed away?
　It colors future years,
And brings its faithful harvest home
　In gladness or in tears.

It spreads itself in coming days
　Through all time's folio pages;
Aye, overleaps the bounds of time,
　And strikes through endless ages.
Then set your marble pillar up
　Without one chiselled word,
And let some faithful angel-hand
　The solemn truth record.

The fifty years that next shall come,
  If it might be God's will,
Who can restrain his chastened wish
  To see its course fulfil?
Oh, what a fertile future lies
  Within your raptured vision,
Of scenes as bright as prophet eyes
  Have seen in faith's elysian,

A nation brought forth in a day,
  Cannons laid up to rust,
Enfranchised freemen now bear sway,
  And keep their holy trust.
The gospel's healing, saving power,
  As by the heavenly dove,
Makes earth resemble heaven once more,
  With balmy breath of love.

Once, ' twas a great advance to write
  Those thirteen states but one;
On fustian flag to stream aloft
  "E pluribus unum."
But clear as man may spell or guess
  Our future' destiny,
One flag must rule the continent
  Of wide America.

By that Columbus who refused
  On any Sabbath-day
To leave a port however urged
  Upon the briny way;
By the pure pilgrims who refused
  To leave the moored May Flower
On the Lord's day, when drifted here
  From persecution's power;

By the blest spirits of the dead
  Made perfect in the skies;
By the best hopes of freedom's sons
  In future years to rise;
By the prized favor of that God,
  With whom we have to do;
Revere His name, His Sabbaths keep,
  And love His precepts too.

Your venerated fathers now
  Stand trembling o'er the grave,
And, under God, they look to you
  Fair virtue's form to save.
They'd have you plant inverted trees,
  Whose roots embrace the sun,
As soon as hope for freedom's growth
  Where Christian faith's foregone.

Ye churches of the living God,
  Ye spouse of Christ, our king,
Ye noble band of Wesley's faith,
  With us your tribute bring.
'Tis Heaven's almighty power and grace
  That kept you in the way;
'Tis God's commanding voice you hear
  Work while it's called to-day.

Ye wasting forms of ripened age,
  We hope your days may last
Till many blooming Junes have come,
  And autumn fruits have passed;
And when your dust is garnered up—
  This soon, alas, must be—
May you in Christ be satisfied
  With an immortal day.

Ye budding youth and manhood's prime,
  Your weaver-shuttle days
Will fill the warp of life too soon
  To yield to sinful ways.
Then make through grace, your calling sure,
  For so the word is given,
And thread a course so angel pure
  'Twill terminate in Heaven.

The Choir then sung the following

THANKSGIVING HYMN.

I.

We plow the fertile meadows, and sow the furrow'd land;
But yet the waving harvest depends on God's own hand;
It is his mercy gives us the sunshine and the rain,
That paints with verdant beauty the mountain and the plain.
  Every blessing we enjoy, comes to us from God:
  Then praise his name, then praise his name,
  For he is ever good, for he is ever good.

II.

By him were all things fashioned around us and afar;
He made the earth and ocean, and every shining star;
He made the pleasant spring-time, the summer bright and warm,
The golden days of autumn, the winter and the storm.
  Every blessing we enjoy, &c.

III.

He makes the glorious sunset, the moon to sail on high;
He bids the breezes fan us, and thundering clouds to fly;
He gives us every blessing, to him our lives we owe.
Every blessing we enjoy, &c.

The audience was entertained by the exhibition of a few household relics; an old chair belonging to Capt. JOSHUA FOBES, and brought by him into the country at the settlement of the Township; a kitchen table belonging to WARREN GIDDINGS, manufactured by his father, JOSHUA GIDDINGS, forty-seven years ago from timber split from logs, with only a broadax and chisel.

Rev. ALVIN COE* being present, made some interesting statements, among which the fact was noticed, that he preached the first sermon in the first meeting house in the Township, which was a spacious log building, warmed by a fire in the center.

During the day and evening several anecdotes were related of early life, and *battles* of the early settlers with bruin.

The Ancient Choir then sung the following hymn to the tune of *Greenfield:*—

I.

I'll praise my maker with my breath;
And when my voice is lost in death,
 Praise shall employ my nobler powers:
My days of praise shall ne'er be past,
While life, and thought, and being last,
 Or immortality endures.

II.

How blest the man whose hopes rely
On Israel's God; He made the sky,
 And earth and seas with all their train:
His truth forever stands secure,
He saves the oppressed, He feeds the poor,
 And none shall find his promise vain.

At the close of the morning exercises, the weather promising a fair afternoon, the meeting was adjourned to meet at half past twelve o'clock in the Grove of HORI MINER, when the Marshals

---
*Since deceased.

proceeded to form a procession, which proceeded to Lindenville in the following order:

1. MARSHALS.
2. OFFICERS.
3. SPEAKERS, CHAPLAIN AND EDITORS.
4. PIONEER GUESTS.
5. INVITED GUESTS.
6. ANCIENT CHOIR (drawn by two yoke of oxen).
7. WAYNE CHOIR.
8. CITIZENS OF WAYNE.
9. PERSONS FROM ABROAD.

Where, after partaking of refreshments, proceeded to the Grove, when the afternoon exercises commenced by singing by the Choir.

Joyful, joyful, joyful be our numbers, &c.

Golden hours have fleeted like a spell,
And now we're called to part and bid farewell.
Give the hand of friendship, ere we part,
May heaven now embalm it on each heart.

At the commencement of the address of J. R. GIDDINGS, he called for all the old soldiers present who fought in the War of 1812 to rise; twenty-one arose.

ADDRESS.

Mr. President:—Standing between the eternity of the past, and that of the future, we look to one for instruction, and the other for the consummation of all our hopes. We turn our thoughts back upon the scenes of childhood and youth, as the most precious jewels contained in the treasures of memory. When age creeps upon us, we love to gaze upon the delightful landscape over which we carelessly traveled in early life; and as it fades in the twilight of increasing years, " distance lends enchantment to the view."

With emotions like these, I now look back upon the early settlement of our township. At the age of ten years I became a resident upon her territory, now called " Wayne." All around me was then novel and interesting. Every incident of that period made a strong impression upon my mind, and I think but few of the interesting events of that period have escaped from my memory.

I was in some degree associated with the pioneers; I witnessed the obstacles which they encountered, and the difficulties which they overcame; I mingled with them in their toils; I participated with them in their privations, and shared with them the hardships of that early period of our settlement. In discharging the duty assigned me on the present occasion, it will be my highest ambition to narrate historical facts. They will be familiar to a portion of the audience, but my object will be to place them on record, in order that they may be read by our descendents in coming time.

Before entering upon the incidents, of the first settlement of Wayne, I beg leave to refer to some antecedents connected with the history of the Western Reserve.

By the terms of the original Charter, granted by the crown of England to the Colonists, their territory extended to the Pacific Ocean. Other Colonies held similar claims. These conflicting titles were compromised in 1787. After the Revolution had rendered these Colonies " independent States,' it became necessary that all conflict of jurisdiction should be adjusted upon a permanent basis. Accordingly the State of Connecticut released to the United States all jurisdiction over the territory west of her present boundaries; *reserving* her interest in the soil of all that " tract of country within our territory, lying north of the completion of the forty-first degree of latitude, bounded east by the west line of the State of Pennsylvania, and extending west one hundred and twenty miles." It was this emphatic language used in the deed of cession which gave to this country the name of the Western *Reserve*.

In the year 1796, Seth Pease, Esq., then of Washington City, was employed by the United States to establish the southern boundary of the territory thus reserved by the State of Connecticut. He performed this duty by first ascertaining with great precision the point at which the completion of the forty-first degree, north latitude, intersects the Pennsylvania line. He then extended this boundary line west some forty miles during that season.

In 1797, this eastern part of the Reserve was laid off into townships, or rather some of the north and south lines which separate the tiers of townships, were run from the boundary line north to the Lake Shore. These lines were five miles distant from each other, and the eastern range of townships lying on the State line was called the "*first range;*" the next was called the "second range;" thus rising in number as they continued west until they reached the "twenty-fourth range," that being the western tier of townships.

In 1798, the east and west lines which separate the different townships were run, at five miles distant from each other, commencing on the State line and running west. The southern tier was " numbered *one;*" the next tier was "numbered *two;*" thus rising in number as they continued north. By this description of " number" and " range", the geographical location of each township was ascertained, and that which is now called " *Wayne* " was for many years know only as township " No. eight, in the second range."

In the month of June, 1798, Titus Hayes, then a young man of unusual energy, left Hartland in the State of Connecticut with the intention of joining a company of Surveyors, to be employed on the Reserve during that season. He came by the way of Canandaigua, in the State of New York, with no other companion than a faithful dog, and with his gun, a loaf of bread, and some salt in his knapsack, he left Erie, in the State of Pennsylvania. At a place called Livingston, in the county of Crawford, he passed the last cabin, and trusting to his pocket compass, he bore southwesterly, and entered the State of Ohio, near the south-east corner of Richmond, passing through the territory now called Andover; he entered this township near the north-east corner; he swam the Pymatuning Creek, near the corner of lot twenty-eight, on which Samuel Jones, Sr., now resides. He often assured your speaker that he then admired the beautiful lands in the neighborhood where he subsequently settled, and that he then formed the determination to purchase and cultivate a portion of them. It is an interesting fact, that he must have passed near, if not over, the grounds now appropriated to the cemetery, where his body was buried nearly fifty years afterward. His was the first visit of civilized man to the interior of our township.

It was then an unbroken wilderness. The dark umbrage of the forest protected the virgin soil from the noontide rays. The cool waters flowed quietly along these beautiful rivulets. All was then quiet, and Nature reigned in all her pristine loveliness.

In 1799, the township was surveyed into lots of a half mile square, each containing one hundred and sixty acres. In 1800, by deeds of partition among the proprietors of the "Connecticut Land Company," the township was conveyed to Oliver Phelps, Esq., of Canandaigua, one of the original members of said Company.

HISTORY OF THE HARPERSFIELD TRACT.

In 1801, Oliver Phelps conveyed two thousand eight hundred and eleven acres, being a tract of one mile in width from the north side of the Township, to Roswell Hotchkiss, who held it in trustee for an association of individuals, living in the town of Harpersfield, in the State of New York, called the "Harpersfield Land Company." They had purchased of Mr. Phelps, town eleven in the fifth range, now called Harpersfield, and as that township was regarded more valuable than others, the tract on the north side of Wayne was put into the contract to reduce it to the average value of the other townships of the Reserve. Hence that part of the town was for forty years known by the name of the "Harpersfield Tract."

THE FIRST SETTLEMENT OF WAYNE.

In the spring of 1803, Simon Fobes, Esq. of Somers, in the State of Connecticut, contracted with Oliver Phelps for sixteen hundred acres of land in township No. eight, in the second range. The tract embraced one entire tier of lots lying south of, and adjoining the east and west center line. These lots were numbered from fifty up to and including sixty.

On the 21st of June of that year, Joshua Fobes and his wife Dorothy, accompanied by Elias Fobes, a younger brother of some nine or ten years of age, started from Connecticut with the intention of settling in this township. Their father attended them on their journey with the intention of seeing them located in the wilderness to which they were emigrating. After one or two days travel they were joined by David Fobes, a cousin, who shared with them the hardships and privations of that protracted journey. In forty-nine days they reached Gustavus, and, for the time being, found shelter in the cabin of Jesse Pelton who had settled at the center of the township.

Soon after their arrival they proceeded to ascertain the situation of their lands. This done, the father returned to Connecticut. Joshua Fobes and David commenced chopping timber and preparing a cabin, but the exposure of the journey affected the health of Joshua so much that he could not remove on to his lands until the 8th of October. On that day the family removed into Wayne as it is now called. The family consisted of Joshua Fobes, his wife Dorothy, David Fobes and Elias Fobes. These four farmers were emphatically the "*first settlers of Wayne.*" I may be permitted to remark that now, after the lapse of fifty years, they all live and *are here present.*

The Scripture informs us that "God gave to man dominion over the fish of the sea and the fowl of the air, and over the cattle, and over all the earth." Half a century since, our friends, just referred to, accepted a portion of this donation and took actual possession of so much of the earth as they could then cultivate within this township. They also exercised dominion over all the cattle around them, and over all the fish they could catch, and all the fowls they could bring under their subjection. The cabin in which they lived was near the south-east corner of lot fifty-seven. Here they spent laborious days and lonely nights. Soon after they had settled down in their new house, David Fobes left them and returned to the residence of his father in Massachusetts. Mr. and Mrs. Fobes, with the brother Elias spent the winter of 1803-4, with no civilized neighbor within less than five miles from their dwelling. They were often visited by Indians who lived in the township, and who occasionally supplied them with venison and bear's meat. They were usually friendly; but it may not be out of place to say, that on one occasion two of them visited the cabin of our pioneers, when they found Mrs. Fobes without company, they became boisterous in their demands for whiskey; but she, understanding their habits, refused to furnish it. They drew their knives in a threatening manner; she had recourse to the weapon most used by her sex (the broom-stick) and drove them from the cabin. Often amid the dreary hours of night, they listened to the howling wolf, and the screeching owl, who really appeared to be almost the only social beings about them.

On the west, in the township of Windsor, at the distance of some fifteen miles, were a few families; but there was no road by which they could be visited. On the north, their nearest neighbors were in Kingsville, some twenty miles distant without a road, while on the east there were no settlers nearer than Meadville, Pa. They had no intercourse with white people except at the south. In Gustavus were two or three families, with perhaps as many in Kinsman and Vernon. These constituted their neighbors. With heroic firmness they encountered the solitude, the toils and privations of pioneer life. They cheered us who subsequently arrived; they encouraged us in the midst of difficulties, and stimulated us to further efforts while contending with the obstacles which beset us on every hand. They have witnessed the change that has taken place around them; they have seen the wilderness made " to blossom like the rose," and now, when their sun of life is descending, and the chilling autumn is coming upon them, they find themselves surrounded with the comforts, the luxuries which cluster in their quiet dwellings.

FIRST BIRTH IN THE TOWNSHIP.

On the 21st of April, A. D. 1804, Mrs. Fobes gave birth to a son. He was the first child born in the township. He was named Alvin. In his childhood, his youth, I was well acquainted with him. He was amiable, industrious and enterprising; but died before reaching the meridian of life.

In May 1804, Simon Fobes, Jr., now present, came to this township and took up his residence with his brothers. His presence greatly cheered and comforted them With his society the summer passed off pleasantly; but he returned to Connecticut in the autumn, and our pioneer family was left to spend the second winter without other neighbors than those heretofore referred to.

During the summer of 1804, a wagon road was opened from their residence to Morgan. This road was occasionally traveled, and our pioneers were, at times, called on by the lonely traveler who, in that day, was always delighted to find a cabin amid the dreary wilderness through which he passed.

The next year proved more auspicious to our friends. Early in the season Simon Fobes, Jr., returned to Wayne. He came in a wagon drawn by two horses, which enabled him to bring with him many articles of clothing and other necessaries which the family greatly needed. He was also accompanied by a cousin, Jabez Fobes, who is now present with us. His father had purchased lands in Wayne, and the son came to rear a cabin and prepare a place for his father's family. These were joyful tidings to our lonely pioneers, and they imparted fresh hope and kindled new expectations in the breasts of those who had begun to despond.*

By hard labor they cleared several acres of land. On this they planted a garden and corn, and had sowed a small field of wheat. Indeed, they were beginning to raise a supply of provisions for their own support.

---

* During the winter of 1804-5, some friends in Gustavus advised Mr. Fobes to leave his cabin and remove to some of the settlements south. He submitted the proposition to Mrs. Fobes, who, with true heroism, declared she would live and die in the township in which they were located.

During the winter of 1804-5, Titus Hayes and Elisha Giddings removed from Canandaigua, in the State of New York, with their families on sleds drawn by oxen. They reached Hartford, in the County of Trumbull, in the month of March. Here they remained during the season, engaged in raising corn and getting a stock of provisions for the next season, intending to settle in this township during the following autumn. Accordingly, on the 8th of October, these gentlemen and their families removed to Wayne, and took up their residence in a cabin, erected on lot thirty-three, which Mr. Hayes had purchased of Oliver Phelps.

Mr. Fobes and family had resided in the township just two years before the arrival of any other family. Elisha Giddings soon erected a cabin and removed to lot thirty-four where his brother Joseph W. Giddings now resides. The arrival of these families was an auspicious event to our pioneers. The gloom which had brooded around them for two years was broken, and the dawnings of social life began to cheer their pathway. It is true, the " new settlers" were more than two miles distant from them; but at that period families resident within two miles of each other were regarded as " conversant neighbors."

In the autumn of 1805, George Wakeman, a farmer on the Yohoghany, in Westmoreland county, Pennsylvania, came to this township and purchased lot eighty-five, and employed a man to make some improvement thereon.

During the autumn of that year, Joshua Giddings, father of your speaker, also purchased several lots of land in different parts of the township. Jabez Fobes also erected a small cabin during the autumn on lot eighty-eight, and commenced felling timber near where Mr. Dean now resides.

Edward Inman, of Somers, in the State of Connecticut, also made a purchase of lands here during the autumn, and prepared to move his family on to them. But the winter of 1805-6 found only three families actually resident in the township. These families consisted of ten persons, beside two unmarried men, Simon Fobes, Jr., and Jabez Fobes, and the boy Elias Fobes, making in all, thirteen souls. Of the six married persons referred to, all are now living and present, except Titus Hayes. He lived to see our township settled

with a numerous population, and himself respected and honored
with important trusts. He died, however, in the midst of apparent
usefulness. There were also five children beside the two young
men, all of whom are now living, and now present, except Alvin
Fobes, to whom I have previously referred.

In the winter of 1805-6, Joshua Giddings, accompanied by his
son Aranda P., came from Canandaigua and commenced an
improvement near the center of the town on lot forty-five. Here
they erected a cabin, and planted a small field of corn and a garden.

In the month of May, George Wakeman with his family, his
son-in-law, Henry Moses and family, removed into Wayne, and
settled upon lot eighty-five.

In the same month the family of Joshua Giddings, consisting of
his wife Elizabeth, his son Joseph W., and your humble speaker,
who was the youngest of the family, left Canandaigua in charge of
Nathaniel Coleman, at that time recently married. His wife, a
sister of your speaker, and himself constituting a separate family.
We reached Conneaut on the 16th of June, a day rendered
memorable by the total eclipse of the sun. Coming down the old
salt road which ran near the center of the first range of towns
nearly to the south line of Williamsfield, we cut a road across the
farm now occupied by Capt. Stanhope, and reached the Pymatuning at the point where the bridge on the south road in Wayne now
stands. Here we descended to the low bottom lands, and following
down the stream until we passed the mouth of the small creek
which empties in from the west, we forded the creek, then turning
to the right, we crossed the small stream, and ascended a handsome
plateau, where we found an Indian wigwam. Here we halted for
the night. It was near the close of a beautiful day in June, just
as the sun was casting its last lingering rays upon the tops of the
trees on the high grounds east of us, that we unyoked our oxen and
took possession of the desolated wigwam. Here we ate our suppers,
and found our first night's lodging in the township of our future
residence. Ours was the first wagon that crossed the " Pymatuning" in Wayne, and the sixth family that settled within its
territory. The next morning, being the 22d of June, we resumed
our journey. Traveling in a westerly direction we passed the

small cabin of Jabez Fobes, near where Mr. Dean's dwelling now stands; around this cabin he had chopped some two or three acres of timber. Traveling to the north of west, we entered upon the road leading from Gustavus to Morgan where it passed over a part of lot sixty-five. We stopped at the residence of Mr. Fobes for an hour, and then passed on to the cabin erected by my father and brother on lot forty five where we commenced our residence. Our cabin contained but one room, without hearth or chimney, or window. Our furniture had been left at Buffalo, to be forwarded by water. We were without chairs or table; with only such materials for cooking as were deemed necessary for us on our journey.

Mr. Coleman soon after commenced an improvement on lot sixty-five near the center line of the township, where he subsequently settled.

About the 1st of July, Edward Inman and family, with his son Edward, Jr., and family, arrived and settled on lot eighty-six. Soon after this, Nathan Fobes and family reached the township and took up their residence in the cabin prepared for them by Jabez Fobes on lot eighty-eight. Thus, at the commencement of the winter of 1806-7, there were ten families actually resident in the township, beside David Fobes, Jabez Fobes, Simon Fobes, Jr., Samuel Phillips and Stephen Inman, who were unmarried men. The whole population at that time according to my recollection, numbered forty-seven souls.

FIRST SABBATH MEETING FOR PUBLIC WORSHIP.

Soon after our family became residents of the township, my father proposed a meeting of the people for public worship on the Sabbath. Having consulted with his neighbors, he appointed a meeting at his cabin. I think it was held on the second Sabbath in July. At the proper hour all the inhabitants of the township, clad in their best holiday suits, were convened. All were seated on benches prepared for that purpose. The weather was warm. The door was set open, and through it and a window without glass, and the open space left in the roof for the escape of smoke, sufficient light was admitted to render the room pleasant. All were solemn, maintaining a decorum which in that day characterized our meetings for public worship. My father was the only male professor of religion present. He and my brother Elisha Giddings sang a hymn. He then led in prayer. My brother-in-law, Nathaniel Coleman, read a sermon from a volume of sermons by the Rev. Mr. Storrs, of Somers, Connecticut; another prayer and another hymn closed the services of the day. Those present appeared devout and conscious that they were establishing habits and laying the moral foundations of a community that would continue long after they and their children, and their children's children would sleep in dust. The practice thus introduced was continued for many years, nor was it suspended until a regular Church and Society were formed, and a regular Pastor ordained to lead them in spiritual matters.

FIRST SABBATH PREACHING.

In the published memoirs of the "Rev. Joseph Badger," it is stated that he preached at the house of Joshua Fobes in Wayne, on the 2nd day of November, A. D., 1806, which he states to have been the first "Sabbath Preaching" in this town. I well recollect the circumstance, having myself carried to some families the intelligence of Mr. Badger's arrival on Saturday, and his intention to preach the next day. The weather was not favorable, however, and but a portion of the people convened to hear the sermon.

Early in the spring of 1807, Nathaniel Coleman moved into his cabin. During the summer, Stephen Feather with his family settled upon lot eighty-seven, on which Mr. Smilie now resides. And Mr. Partridge with his family moved on to lot ninety-six, now occupied by Mr. Sheldon.

In November, Simon Fobes, Esq., removed his family to Wayne, and resided for the winter with his son, Joshua. He also brought with him his aged parents, so that four generations, constituting three families, actually resided at the same time in one cabin. Thus we commenced the winter of 1807-8, with thirteen families actually resident in our township.

This was, however, a very unpropitious season for the settlers. The rains were so frequent that they could not clear lands, and consequently could not plant corn for their support. The rains were attended with an unusual amount of lightning, which appeared to have but little effect in relieving the atmosphere of electricity.

During this season the inhabitants found it necessary to erect a bridge and causeway over the Pymatuning Creek and swamp, where the south road now crosses that stream. It was a gigantic undertaking for the number of people engaged in it. It was, however, effected by the voluntary labors of the thirteen families then resident in the township; although it was a work, when compared with the ability of the inhabitants, far greater than it would now be to build a railroad through it.

During this season the Messrs. Gillis, of Kinsman, succeeded in getting their grist mill in operation. It was regarded as a matter of great public interest, inasmuch as it afforded the public increased facilities for the grinding of grain.

THE FIRST DEATH AND FUNERAL.

On the 4th of February, 1808, Mrs. Thankful Fobes, grandmother of Joshua Fobes, died suddenly at his home. It was the first death in the township, and appeared to impress our people with a feeling of deep solemnity. It then became necessary to decide upon the location of a cemetery. And Simon Fobes, Jr., Joshua Fobes, Titus Hayes and Elisha Giddings met at my father's cabin and with him proceeded to select a suitable location for a graveyard. Mr. Hayes proposed to donate the land. It was then an unbroken wilderness. The site agreed upon was some little distance out of the center of the town and is still occupied as a burial place. The location for the grave being fixed, Simon Fobes, Jr., and his brother Levi, commenced digging it. John L. Cook, of Kinsman, made the coffin, and the funeral was attended with great solemnity. There was no clergyman present; but a suitable sermon was read, with appropriate prayers and singing, and the body was deposited in its final resting place amid the lonely forest. The day was cold and dreary. The snow covered the earth; the trees having put off their foliage, stood exposed to the chilling blasts, and nature around us appeared emblematical of the death which had called us together.

Three days subsequently we attended the funeral of Simon

Fobes, her husband. He was buried beside his deceased wife in our forest grave yard.

The year 1808 was the only season in which the early settlers of Wayne suffered from the scantity of food. The wet season of the previous year, as already stated, had prevented them from raising their usual supply of corn. As early as May or June there was great demand for flour, corn and potatoes. But these articles were all of them difficult to obtain. No flour was to be had short of "Beaver Falls," in the State of Pennsylvania; and many of our settlers were too destitute of the "root of all evil" to obtain "the staff of life." Few of them had become expert hunters; yet much of their food was obtained from the forest.

Soon as the wheat was so far perfected as to be separated from the chaff it was cut in small quantities and used for food. I think every family had a supply of milk, and that article really constituted the principal support of some. It may be regarded as mortifying to the descendants of some families, were I to state that their ancestors were actually in want of bread. I was myself one of those who actually suffered from hunger, and I well recollect of hearing a neighbor, one who was bowed down with age, say he had not tasted bread for several weeks, and that he had become too weak to labor. But at length new wheat, new potatoes and green corn brought relief, and cheerfulness and hope again were visible among the settlers.

Another misfortune befell our people. Most of the lands which had been purchased in town, were found to have been mortgaged by Oliver Phelps, prior to their sale. Phelps died about this time, and his estate being insolvent, the purchasers were left without remedy. Joshua Giddings felt this loss so severely, that he left the township and settled in Williamsfield.

During this season Messrs. Fobes finished their saw-mill on lot fifty-five. The completion of this mill marked an era in our settlement. From that time we obtained boards for all the various uses to which they are commonly applied. Our dwellings were rendered comfortable by improved floors; partitions were erected to separate bed-rooms from our kitchens, and the people began to think they were enjoying the luxuries of an old settlement.

The commencement of the year 1809 was marked, like that of its predecessor by two deaths. On the 13th of January, an infant daughter of Nathaniel Coleman died, and on the 21st of that month his wife SUBMIT, only sister of him who now addresses you, departed this life. She was the first person who died in the township at an age to be useful. They too were buried in our forest cemetery. This is not an occasion on which it would become me to speak of that loved sister. Our hearts were bound to her by the strongest possible attachment, and although forty-five years have passed since she bade us adieu, yet I often find the tear of affection bathing my cheek when I reflect upon that parting scene. These were the only deaths which occured in our township during the first ten years of its settlement.

During the year 1809, there was no increase of our settlement by immigration. A portion of the people were engaged in efforts to repurchase the land bought of Mr. Phelps. They also opened roads, improved their dwellings, and some of our young men were married, and erected cabins, and commenced improvements. Joshua Fobes removed his family on to lot fifty-five, where his brother Levi now resides. Nathaniel Coleman commenced an improvement on lot seventy, where he now lives; Samuel Phillips, being married, moved on to lot ninety, where he erected a cabin, near the present residence of William Matthews; David Fobes, being married, also erected a cabin, and settled on the farm where he still resides.

During the autumn of that year, a school-house was erected near the centre of the town. It was a small log cabin, with windows of oiled paper. It has not been visible, I think, for the last twenty years. Keziah Jones, now the wife of Nathaniel Coleman, was employed to teach the first school taught in the township. Your speaker was a member of that school, and in it obtained the only common school education which he acquired after he was ten years of age.

During the year 1811, our settlement began to increase more rapidly. Samuel Jones removed from Connecticut, and settled on lot twenty-eight, where he still lives; James W. Foster also erected a cabin, and removed on to lot thirteen, on which Anson Jones now resides.

Samuel Wakeman, son of George Wakeman, removed to Wayne, and commenced an improvement on the lot on which his father resided. There were, according to my recollection, seventeen families in Wayne Township at the commencement of the year 1812. During the year 1812, our settlement made but little advance. The war of that year occupied the public attention. In that war, Wayne, like other portions of the country, participated. We were then attached to Trumbull county for military purposes. The townships of Wayne and Gustavus constituted a company, commanded by our respected pioneer, Joshua Fobes. When the news of General Hull's surrender of Detroit reached us, the whole of our regiment was ordered to take the field. It is forty-one years, this day, since our regiment met in general rendezvous at Kinsman, and on the same day took up its line of march for the frontier. Most of that gallant band, commanded by Col. Richard Hayes, of Hartford, were then in the pride and glory of manhood. Health marked each cheek, and valor sat upon each brow. *Forty-one years have passed.* Our commander and many more of those gallant spirits have departed to their final rest. Others remain, and are now present. In order that the audience may witness specimens of the soldiers of that day, I respectfully ask each member of Hayes' Regiment, who met with us on the 24th of August, A. D. 1812, to rise in his place.

[All the officers and soldiers present complied with this request, and stood in their places, when the speaker resumed.]

Thanks, fellow soldiers, for this opportunity of looking upon faces long since familiar. Time has made his mark upon us all. Our cheeks are furrowed; our heads are grey; our hands are palsied and trembling; the elasticity of youth has departed. *We are old men!* To many of us this will be our last interview. Let all of us be able to say at the close of our moral warfare, " *We have fought the good fight.*"

Fellow citizens, pardon this digression. It was prompted by feelings common to our nature. I will resume the narrative of facts.

After two days' march, one-half of our troops were discharged and returned home. Capt. Fobes, being one of the senior officers of his grade, continued in the field for some three months, when the militia were relieved by regular troops and drafted men. He was attended by many of his neighbors. All, I believe, performed their duty with fidelity and honor, and all returned in safety save one. Nathan Fobes, Jr., died on his way home in February following. He was included in the draft, and remained in service six months. He fell a victim to the exposures and hardships of that campaign. He was my early friend. Sincere, warm-hearted and brave, he left us at the threshold of his manhood. We mourn the loss and cherish the memory of our young and gallant companion in arms.

The disease called the "epidemic of 1812," which proved so fatal in many parts of the country, appeared in Wayne near the close of that year.

The cases, however, were few, and it had so far lost its malignant form, that it disappeared from among us without a fatal termination in any instance. The people of our township commenced the year 1813 under favorable auspices.

I have endeavored to sketch the progress of our settlement for ten years from its commencement. Since that period it has advanced more rapidly. At the present time there is one or more settlers on every original lot in the township.

In 1850 its population numbered 899 actual residents; 232 were charged with tax on real estate. There were 6,751 acres under cultivation, and the whole value of real and personal estate was estimated at $276,746. There were raised within the township, 7,150 bushels of corn; 3,600 bushels of wheat, and there were 22,525 pounds of sugar manufactured. The produce of cheese was 334,400 pounds, and 33,460 pounds of butter were exported by our farmers.

The devotion of our people to the cause of education may be estimated from the facts that they had, in 1850, seven common schools, one academy, ten teachers and two hundred and ninety-eight pupils. Of the persons over twenty-one years of age thirteen were unable to read and write. Only one of them, however, was a native of the township, and *unfortunate* in point of mental endowments.

Of the morality of our people, I can say there has been very little litigation among them. I think I can say that in fifty years the whole number of law suits carried to the Court of Common Pleas from this township, has not averaged one to each five years. I am not aware that any resident of the township was ever arrested for crime; indeed, if any have been indicted for even minor offences, such as assault and battery, the fact has escaped my recollection, although I have, for more than thirty years, been engaged in the practice of law, and must have been aware of it at the time.

INDUSTRIAL HABITS OF THE PIONEERS.

Our early settlers were men of great energy of character. They were usually drawn to the west by a spirit of enterprise, and they manifested the most determined perseverance. No obstacles daunted them, no privations deterred them from the accomplishment of their purpose. The rugged forests were overcome only by the steady, untiring energies of an industrious people. Severe and constant labor seemed to be regarded by them as mere recreation. At early dawn they were engaged in felling the forest trees, and they only retired when the darkness of evening constrained them to leave their labors. In the autumn, they were usually engaged in clearing off their fallow. At that season they might have been found at their labor, "throwing in their log-heaps" by the light of their fires, long before the first rays of the morning gave evidence of approaching day; and at evening, too, you might have found them engaged in the same employment, long after daylight had ceased to aid them.

During the winter, they usually rose, performed their domestic duties, ate their breakfasts, and · were ready to enter upon field labor so soon as daylight would permit. Each family manufactured sugar from the sap of the maple. It constituted almost the only article of commerce with which they could purchase such necessaries as were regarded indispensible for the use of the family; the season of sugar-making was, therefore, one of hard and unusual toil, as well as of exposure to the cold and wet weather. Gathering sap and chopping wood occupied the day, and during both night and day the kettles were kept boiling. Often from Monday morning till

Saturday night, the fires were not permitted to die away; indeed, the Sabbath was not at all times a day of rest among those employed in making sugar. By an examination of the records of Grand River Presbytery, it will be seen that at a comparatively recent period, that body expressed their disapprobation of gathering sap on the Sabbath day by its members.

Our roads in that day were bad, and uncomfortable in the extreme sense of those terms. At this time they would be regarded as impassable. The deep mud, short turns, the obstructions of logs and other inequalities, rendered them unsuited to the use of horses, and oxen were our only beasts of draft. When the pioneer was compelled to visit the older settlements for provisions or for grinding his grain, he took his oxen and wagon, never forgetting his bell. Whenever and wherever night overtook him, he would stop, unyoke his oxen, put his bell on one of them, and permit them to go forth to obtain their food in nature's pasture. The faithful animals appeared conscious of the trust reposed in them, for they seldom rambled out of hearing of their owner. In the morning he would eat his own frugal meal, yoke his oxen and resume his journey. His return was always hailed with pleasure by his family, who were usually in want of the necessaries he brought with him, and anxious for his safety.

Nor were the females less industrious. In summer and winter, in autumn and spring, they were engaged in their duties of preparing food and manufacturing raiment for themselves and families. They often dressed the flax after it had been broken, always hatcheled and spun it, and carded and spun the tow which it yielded. They made not only their own ordinary apparel, but colored a portion of the yarn or thread, and wove their cloth in checks, from which they made up their holiday dresses; pocket handkerchiefs were fabricated in the same manner.

They colored the wool from a dye made from the bark of the butternut tree, tinctured with copperas; they carded, spun, and wove it; they then cut and made the garments for their fathers, brothers and husbands. I need not remind the old men now present of the buzzing wheel which so often awoke us in the autumnal mornings long before the early dawn awoke the feathered songsters in the forests around our dwellings.

The garments thus manufactured, were regarded as well suited to the wants of that day. I may be permitted to say, that I first appeared as an Attorney and Counselor before the Supreme Court of our State, in shirt and pants spun and wove, cut and made in my own dwelling.

PRIVATIONS AND ECONOMY.

Our early settlers were subjected to many privations, as would appear from what has already been stated. Their dwellings were rude and inconvenient. Glass windows were not to be enjoyed at that day. The light was obtained usually from the chimney, the door, and window places filled with oiled paper instead of glass. They had usually but one room, which served as a kitchen, dining room, parlor and nursery. Their crockery was arranged on shelves in one corner of the house, and under these shelves their iron ware and cooking materials were arranged. They used their chamber, also, for a sleeping apartment, the storing of provisions and such other articles as were deemed worthy of a place in the dwelling. The roofs were formed of clapboards split from oak timber. They generally conducted off the rain pretty well, but in winter, when the wind blew, the snow would find its way between these clapboards, and it was not unusual for those lodging "upstairs" to awake in the morning and find half an inch of snow on their couches. The mode of ascending into the chamber, was usually by a common ladder, or by means of large wooden pins driven into the logs at proper distances, on which the person could step while ascending.

Their wardrobe was usually in keeping with their dwellings, coarse in their texture, and of the plainest kind. At first, we had neither fulling mills nor tailors, and while I would speak to the mortification of no one, I may say that for more than two years I was myself destitute of a coat of fulled cloth in which I could appear at church, and I was more than twenty-two years of age when I obtained my first suit of broadcloth. Others were more fortunate than myself, while others were less successful in that respect. It was common, in the early period of our settlement for gentlemen to appear at church on the Sabbath bare-footed, in clean shirts, pants, and vests, without coats, which, sometimes were not *conveniently to be had.* Our ladies were generally in the habit of walking to church bare-footed, carrying their shoes and stockings in their hands until near the place of meeting, when they would stop and clothe their pedestrial extremities, and then walk into the sanctuary. After services, they would again preserve both stockings and shoes, by carrying them home in their hands. All, however, were clad in neat apparel, and for that day their garments were regarded as decent.

The food was somewhat of the same character. Wheat was scarce, and it was impossible at times to obtain grinding. Most families were provided with "samp mortars." These were formed by burning a cavity into the top of a stump, and then providing a large pestle, six or eight feet in length, suspended over the stump, by fastening the upper end to a spring-pole, the lower end being suited to the cavity in the stump below it. Some fifteen inches from the lower end, two pins protruded from opposite sides, which served as handles. The corn being placed in the cavity of the stump, the pestle was brought down on it with such force as to break it in pieces, and a woman or child would pound sufficient for the family a meal in a very short time. Potatoes were also much used. Often have I seen a family gathered around the table at dinner, with no other variety of food than boiled potatoes, salt and butter. Pastry was little used. The first "minced pies" I ate on the Reserve, were composed of pumpkin instead of apple, vinegar in the place of wine or cider, bear's meat instead of beef. The whole was sweetened with wild honey instead of sugar, and seasoned with domestic peppers, pulverized, instead of cloves, cinnamon and allspice, and never did I taste pastry with a better relish.

THEIR HOSPITALITY.

The pioneer felt himself at home wherever he found a cabin. He was always made welcome. He and his team were treated with precisely the same fare that his host and his team enjoyed. If he reached a cabin near nightfall, he was expected to remain until the next morning. His visits were interesting. He informed his friends of all that had happened in his region, the progress of the settlement, the prospect of its increase, the crops, and all the incidents of the day; the last arrival from Connecticut or York State was told, and events which had transpired in those States a month previously were listened to with interest, as the latest news of the day. Nor was the guest expected to hurry away in the morning. He remained until after breakfast, when he departed with the kind wishes of his friends, whom he never offended by offering pay for his entertainment.

If a pioneer visited his neighbor, he was always invited to remain and partake of the usual repast of the family. In that day temperance societies had not been formed. Ardent spirits were in common use. They were sometimes found in cabins destitute of flour and meat. They were regarded as approximating to the necessaries of life. The hospitality of that day demanded their presentation to every visitant. They were used at all social gatherings, at the raisings of cabins and military musters. I mention these facts with regret, in order that the habits and customs of the early settlers may be accurately known to those who come after us.

THEIR SOCIAL HABITS.

Our pioneers met but seldom for social pleasures. But that circumstance added interest to their gatherings. The ladies did not call at 4 o'clock, P. M., as at this day; they left home in the morning, taking their children with them, and occupied the day in an efficient visit, and in returning before the disappearance of daylight. Never have I seen visits enjoyed with greater zest. In the winter time, when the sledding was good, the oxen were yoked and the entire family took passage in a sled, and the long winter evenings were not unfrequently spent in social conversation among two, three, or sometimes half a dozen families. The friendships of that day were strong and uninterrupted. There were no feuds, no contentions, no strifes among them.

THE FIRST WEDDING IN TOWN.

In the winter of 1807, Philemon Brockway was married to Sarah Fobes, daughter of Nathan Fobes. The marriage was solemnized at the house of her father, and as nearly as I now recollect, all the grown people in town were invited as guests. For weeks the event was looked to as one of unusual interest. Fortunately the snow was some ten inches deep, and the sledding good. With the exception of some aged people, every gentleman and lady who had been invited, was promptly in attendance. It was truly a jovial party. The attendance of a clergyman could not easily be obtained, and a Justice of the Peace was employed to officiate. All passed off merrily. The bride and bridegroom were duly congratulated, and saluted with a friendly kiss. The whiskey king was passed round in earthen bowls and tin cups. Neither goblets nor tumblers were then used among the democratic population of our town. All were social, all were merry, and at a seasonable hour the guests departed to their homes, highly gratified with the "first wedding in town," and it was long referred to as one of the interesting incidents of our early settlement.

ABORIGINAL INHABITANTS.

Some eight or ten families of natives were for many years occupants of a small village situated on the east bank of the Pymatuning creek, on lot ninety-one. It was a delightful situation, overlooking the lowlands along the stream for a great distance above and below the village. The whole population may have numbered forty. They were under the guidance of a shrewd and talented chief named "Omic." They constituted a portion of the Massasauga band of Chippewa tribe. Their sugar camps were in Cherry Valley, whither they repaired every winter for the purpose of making sugar, which they usually carried to Pittsburg for sale. They often furnished our people with venison and bears' meat in return for potatoes and such other articles as our people could spare.

I have no dates relative to the time when those people took up their residence at said village. In 1810 the inhabitants of Williamsfield and Wayne called together and erected a school-house for their accommodation, and a dwelling house for the missionary who undertook to instruct them. These buildings were some seventy rods north-east of the village, and perhaps an equal distance from the south road passing east and west, through the Township.

The name of the missionary was William Matthews. He was uncle to the gentleman of that name, now residing on the road referred to, east of the creek. He commenced teaching the children of the Indians, and appeared to be gaining their confidence, when, unfortunately, the "small pox" made its appearance among them, and several of their number fell victims to that pestilential disease. They regarded this misfortune as an evidence that the "Great Spirit" was not pleased with their location, and as soon as they had fully recovered from the disease, they prepared to seek a new home in the west.

They left in the winter of 1810-11, and never returned. They tarried a while in Huron County, where a son of "Omic" murdered a white man, for which he was arrested, tried, and being convicted, was hanged at Cleveland, in June, 1812. "Omic," with his band, joined the British Indians in the war of that year, and mingled in the "battles of the Peninsula," which were fought on the 26th of September. In those contests he actually engaged in conflict with some of his former friends and benefactors from Wayne and Williamsfield.

CIVIL ORGANIZATION.

I have been unable to ascertain the limits of the organized Township to which Wayne was attested at its first settlement; indeed, I am led to think the public works were that time so loosely kept that it would now be difficult to obtain any authentic date on the subject. Our friend Joshua Fobes, informs me that in 1804, he voted at Hartford on the Presidential election of that year.

My first knowledge of the subject was in 1806, where the three number sevens, now constituting Kinsman, Gustavus and Green; the three number eights, now constituting Williamsfield, Wayne and Colebrook, were organized into a Township by the name of "Green." The elections were then held at the house of Judge Kinsman.

In 1811, the county of Ashtabula was organized, and the tier of townships numbered eight, from the state line to the fifth range, now transferred by the statute from Trumbull County to Ashtabula, and the number eights and nines in the first, second and third ranges were organized into a township by the name of "Wayne." This was the first instance that the name of "Wayne" formed a place on the records of our county, and ours was the first township organized by its officers. There were at that time only eight towns in the county, to wit: Wayne, Windsor, Richfield, Jefferson, Salem, Kingsville, Harpersfield and Ashtabula.

The first township election was at the house of Nathan Fobes. Nathaniel Coleman and Samuel Tuttle were elected Justices of the Peace. The first judicial proceeding was held before Justice Coleman at his house. Joseph Coy was the complaining servant, and a Mr. Hutchinson was the defending master. The case arose under the act "concerning apprentices and servants," then in force, and it was regarded as an interesting incident, and nearly all the men and boys of the township came together to attend this solemn Court, being the first in the township of Wayne.

In 1813, the surveyed townships, numbered eight and nine, in the third range, were set off into an organized township, called "Lebanon," and in 1819 the number nines, in the first and second ranges, were organized into a separate township, by the name of Andover. This left the number eights, in the first and second ranges, to constitute the township of Wayne. They remained together until the year 1826, when number eight, in the first range was incorporated by the name of "Williamsfield," and Wayne township retained its proper cognomen, by which it has since been known, and will probably remain known in coming time.

RELIGIOUS ORGANIZATIONS.

In 1808 the church at Vernon was divided, and those professors of religion, who belonged to the Presbyterian and Congregational faith, resident in Kinsman, Gustavus, Williamsfield and Wayne, were organized into a separate church. The preparitory meeting was held, the church was formed, and the sacrament administered in a log barn, built by George Matthews, in the north part of Kinsman. The Rev. Mr. Wick, of Youngtown, was the officiating clergyman.

In 1816 the people of Wayne and Williamsfield, united in erecting a log meeting house, on lot fifty-one, where the Rev. Mr. Roberts now lives. It was furnished with glass windows, a pulpit and singers' gallery. Soon after its erection, the church above referred to was again divided, and those members who lived in Williamsfield and

Wayne, were organized into a separate church, which held its meetings in this house until 1831, when the house was accidently burned. The Rev. Alvin Coe, was the first preacher employed by the new church, and the venerable Ephraim T. Woodruff, now present, was their first settled pastor.

After the loss of their meeting house, the church was again divided, and a new meeting house was erected at the centre of Wayne, in which the church of this town has since worshiped, while that of Williamsfield has occupied a building of their own.

There has also for many years past been a Methodist church organized in Wayne. They have usually held their meetings at some convenient school-house. They are quite respectable in point of numbers, and highly so in the character of its members; but I have been unable to obtain the necessary date to enable me to state the time of its formation, or to give details of its history.

ANCIENT WORK.

Our township contains but one of those works called "ancient fortifications," of which so much has been written, and so little is known. That work was situated on the west side of the Pymatuning Creek, on lot eighty-nine, near where the mill now stands. It had the appearance of having been designed for defence. Its parapet walls were some three feet in height, and on them were found forest trees of the ordinary size. It was evidently erected by the same people, and for the same purpose, as those ancient works, so numerous at the south and west of us, were erected, and which are described with so much accuracy of detail. I will not therefore occupy further time on that subject.

NATURAL HISTORY.

It may be proper that I should state that the animals found here at the first settlement of our township, were such as were common to the "Reserve" generally. The elk and deer were hunted for their meat, they were plenty, and at times were easily obtained. Besides them there were bears, wolves, gray and black foxes, racoon, wild cat, opossum, porcupine, pole-cat, the black, grey, red and ground squirrel. Our streams contained beaver, otter and muskrat. There was also occasionally a panther, but I recollect of only one having been killed within our township, and that was in the winter of 1808. The wild turkey was very common in the early period of our settlement, and furnished much support to our early inhabitants. Wild geese and ducks were also taken occasionally.

The wolves were troublesome. They killed our hogs and sheep, and a warfare was kept up against them, until they were entirely destroyed about the year 1835. The bear and elk also disappeared about that time. The red fox first began to be seen among us in the year 1817; rabbits also made their appearance about that time.

There are some deer and some turkeys yet found in our forests, but they are few, and are seldom taken.

My friends, I have detained you perhaps too long in this relation of historical facts; but I beg you to remember that I have spoken rather for the information of those who come after us, than for the pleasure of those now present. When fifty years hence, the first centennial anniversary shall be celebrated in this town, I desire the speaker who shall address that assembly, to have before him dates, showing what our township *has been* and *now is*. When fifty years more shall have passed away, and our children's children shall assemble to celebrate the anniversary of our first settlement, they will be interested in facts which are too familiar to excite an interest with us.

As we look forward through the vista of coming time, and contemplate that assemblage of our descendants, we are overwhelmed with thought. What number of people will then inhabit our township? What will be their moral, their political, their religious character? What improvements will they have made in the arts and sciences? In all the conveniences and refinements of life? What laws of nature and of nature's God, of which we are ignorant, will be unfolded to them? How far will they have advanced toward that Millennium of which we read, of which we believe and for which we pray? Who will compose that assembly? Who will preside over it? Who will address it? Fifty years will solve those questions; we cannot answer them.

My attachments to this place and its early settlers are those of childhood and of youth. They were interwoven with my early existence and are deeply impressed upon the memory of age. I loved the dark forests which at that period covered those beautiful fields : I wandered along those crystal streamlets with delight : I gazed upon their limpid waters : I looked around me and admired nature as she stood forth, clad in her beautiful robes : I startled the timid deer from his lair: I gazed upon the ferocious wolf, as he fled from me, and laughed at the awkward movements of the rumpless bear, as he clumsily made his way through the dense underbrush. Those scenes are yet dear to memory.

Though a lad I associated with the pioneers. I participated in their cabin-raisings, their military musters and their social circles; I became attached to them ; and although the storms of adversity have since that period raged around me, and the sunshine of prosperity has at times cheered my life, I still cherish those attachments, and the recollection of those early companions, cheers many a, moment which would otherwise be darkened by solitude. Indeed, when I reflect upon those scenes, and call to mind those companions, my mind is overwhelemed by those hallowed emotions which cluster around the memory of early days, and impart sanctity to the relations of long tried and unfaltering friendship.

Some of those early associates have departed to a higher and a happier sphere. Many yet remain, and are here with us. They must feel a conscious satisfaction in having contributed their influence to establish that moral sentiment, to the promotion of that political intelligence, to the formation of that religious character, which has so long distinguished the people of Wayne. Although they will soon leave their present sphere of action, their works will survive, and their influence will be felt long after their names will be forgotten.

Yes, and posterity will improve upon their example. Greater refinement, a higher morality, more exalted religious views will characterize those who follow us. As we look forward and see mankind more intelligent, more exalted, more holy, our hearts swell with gratitude to our Creator: and as we old people are soon to leave this field of labor, we would cheerfully exhort those who survive us, to let their course be *Onward* and *Upward*.

The following original hymn, by Rev. D. H. BABCOCK, was sung:

I.

God of Nations! ever teach us
From what source our blessings come;
If Thou smile, then we shall prosper;
Wayne shall be a happy home.

II.

May no son of this, our mother,
Ever touch the sparkling bowl;
May no lost, no fallen brother,
Ever chain or sell a soul.

III.

Let affection's sacred fountain,
In pure channels ever run;
So that love shall be immortal—
Friendship shall survive the sun.

IV.

By this process earth shall flourish
With the bloom and hues of Heaven.
Every virtue let us nourish
Till a higher life be given.

V.

Friends of Freedom! onward! onward!
Victory yet shall crown the strife,
And the names of men like Giddings,
Fill the nations with new life.

VI.

Names like his the Globe shall compass,
Like a starry belt or zone,
And this lighted glorious pathway,
Be to coming millions known.

The following Resolution, offered by the Rev. E. B. CHAMBERLAIN, was seconded by several voices:

Resolved, That when this meeting adjourn, it adjourn to meet at the Centre Church, at 10 o'clock on the 24th of August, A. D. 1903.

Mr. C. remarked—" In glancing at this Resolution, which is just put into my hand, it seems like presumption to offer it; the tongue falters. Who will be there on that day? Will any of the venerable forms of these early pioneers? None! Will any of the officers or Marshals who have conducted with such signal ability the proceedings of this day be there? Gone! Will any of the middle-aged, now in active life, among the thousands of this thoughtful assembly be there? They, too, will be gone! They who have addressed us? Gone! all gone! But still, there may be a propriety in passing this Resolution. Among the joyous throngs of youth, who are now just stepping upon life's stage, and "rejoicing as a strong man to run a race," there may be some. The blossoms of health and comeliness now cluster thickly on your brow; may heaven protect you in life and virtue; you will there and then rehearse the proceedings of this day." Adopted unanimously.

On motion of CALVIN C. WICK, Esq.,

Resolved, That the proceedings of this Celebration, with the speech of the Hon. J. R. GIDDINGS, and the Poem of Rev. E. B. CHAMBERLAIN, be published in pamphlet form.

The ancient choir then sung the following stanzas, to the tune of *Sherburn:*

> While shepherds watched their flocks by night,
> All seated on the ground,
> The angel of the Lord came down,
> And glory shone around.
>
> "Fear not," said he, for mighty dread
> Had seized their troubled mind,
> "Glad tidings of great joy I bring
> To you and all mankind.

The President of the Day then gave a history of the old Bible above referred to, when the choir sung the following lines:

> This book is all that's left me now! Tears will unbidden start;
> With faltering lip and throbbing brow, I press it to my heart.
> For many generations past, here is our family tree,
> My mother's hands this bible clasped; she, dying, gave it me.
>
> Ah, well do I remember those whose names these records bear,
> Who round the hearth-stone used to close after the evening prayer,
> And speak of what these pages said, in terms my heart would thrill,
> Though they are with the silent dead, here are they living still.
>
> My father read this holy book to brothers, sisters dear,
> How calm was my poor mother's look, who leaned God's word to hear,
> Her angel face—I see it yet! What thronging memories come!
> Again that little group is met within the halls of home.
>
> Thou truest friend man ever knew, thy constancy I've tried,
> Where all were false I found thee true—my counselor and guide.
> The mines of earth no treasures give, that could this volume buy,
> In teaching me the way to live, it taught me how to die.

The following brief address was then made by JOSHUA FOBES, Sr., the first settler of the town:

It does me good to see so many of my good old friends and acquaintances able to attend this meeting, and I hope and trust that the proceedings of this day will be so conducted as to redound to the glory of God, and to the good of the rising generation, showing forth the mighty works of our Heavenly Father. I confess that I take some humble pride in noticing the tokens of respect that our citizens manifest towards the pioneers, and especially my wife and I. Although we were the first in town, no person will say that we were the instigators of this day's uproar. However, I wish them peace and prosperity in this life and that which is to come, and that the best of Heaven's blessings be their reward. The Lord only knows who of this assembly, at the close of fifty years to come will be alive, and able to tell the proceedings, and who they were that took an active part in the exercises of the day.

When I look back fifty years, the time I first stepped foot into this township, chopping the road to the promised land, then a howling wilderness, inhabited only by beasts of prey and men as wild as they, and to think of the afflictions, hardships and sufferings which we have endured, it seems like a dream when one awakes; also how we have been preserved by an overruling hand of Providence, through many dangers, seen and unseen, I am led to wonder that we are yet alive, whilst almost all the first settlers of my acquaintance are gone to the spirit world, but here and there one left. I feel to take shame to myself, and repent in dust and ashes for the ingratitude that I have returned to Almighty God for the manifold blessings that hath been bestowed upon us all our lives long. Our days are almost numbered; we, too, must soon follow them into the eternal world. Brothers, sisters, the time is short; what we do must be done quickly, for the end of all things is at hand; let us be up and doing, standing with our lamps trimmed and burning, waiting for the coming of our blessed Lord and Savior Jesus Christ, for we know not the day nor hour the Son of Man cometh.

A few words to the rising generation, and I have done. My friends, you see me a poor old gray-headed man, worn out by my imprudence, and the infirmaties of old age, just ready to tumble into the grave. I don't ask you to pattern after me. I hope and trust that my faults and imperfections will be forgotten and forgiven both in this life and that which is to come.

It grieves me to see how little regard some people appear to have for the glory of God, and the good of their own souls, for in Him we live, move and have our being; from him we receive every good and perfect gift. I believe our Heavenly Father designed mankind to be happy, and they can be, if they would but try, as they do to get silver and gold. That little word, TRY, well put in execution, will accomplish great and marvelous things. In the last war with Great Britian, Col. Miller was ordered to take a certain British fort; Miller said "I will try!" He did so, and succeeded in taking the fort. I want you to take heed to your ways, how you spend your time and talents, for time is precious. Try to lay up a treasure in Heaven. Remember the Sabbath day to keep it holy. Take the word of God for your guide; let it be your study to become useful; that tells us what mankind are my nature, and what we must be by grace to inherit eternal life. In all your gettings, get wisdom and knowledge, for knowledge is power. The old adage is, if you would have friends, show yourselves friendly; do to others as you would wish to be done by. Avoid vicious company and contention, which genders strife; as far as in you lies, live peaceably with all mankind.

Now let us all so live, that when time with us on earth shall end, we can celebrate the praises of our blessed Redeemer in that world above where trouble shall cease, and harmony shall abound."

At the conclusion of these remarks, notwithstanding the late hour in the afternoon, another "old-fashioned tune" was called for, and the multitude seemed to listen with increased delight, to the *tune* of "*Delight,*" sung to the verse—

No burning heats by day,
Nor blasts of evening air,
Shall take my health away,
If God be with me there;
Thou art my sun,
And thou my shade,
To guard my head,
By night or noon.

This tune was sung in an animated manner, as they seemed to have caught the inspiration of nature, and reproduced the sweet strains they'd sung in "other days."

And when the tremulous tones of this Ancient Band, which seemed endued with more than earthly melody, had died away—

> "Amid the gray old trunks that high in heaven
> Mingle their mossy boughs,"—

The audience arose and united in singing *Old Hundred*, to the following psalm and doxology:

> "Thus far the Lord hath led me on,
> Thus far his power prolonged my days."

Rev. E. T. WOODRUFF, the first settled minister in Wayne, then made a short, but feeling address, but his voice was so feeble that he was not distinctly heard, and pronounced the benediction.

In the evening, a very large audience assembled at an early hour at the First Congregational Church, and the evening was most agreeably spent in listening to anecdotes and statements from early settlers, in listening to some excellent pieces of music from the Wayne choir, accompanied by the organ; and among the exercises of this occasion, the following poem from the Rev. DANIEL H. BABCOCK, of Plymouth, Mass., a native of this place, was read:

> Full fifty years, with all their scenes, have fled
> Since Joshua Fobes his lonely tent here spread ;
> Since to this howling wilderness he came,
> And on the social hearth lit up a flame.
> Full fifty winters, with their drifting snows,
> And fifty summers, blooming as the rose,
> Have to a past eternity been swept,
> Since the first white man here a household kept.
> Those fifty years—who, who alas, can tell
> What smiles have played—what burning tears have fell,
> What plans succeeded, and what hopes have failed !
> What deeds rejoiced in, and what woes bewailed !
>   Like cities on Ohio's panoramic tide,
> These years, these scenes, before my vision glide.
> I see the axe by which the first tree fell ;
> I hear the blow—it echoes through the dell.
> I see the tinder-box, the flint, the steel ;
> The spark now catches, and the flames reveal.
> A genial fire within the forest glows,
> Where, for uncounted years, no flame arose.
> A spot is cleared, a house of logs I see,
> Built by some spring, or brook of joyous glee.

Within that house a family now dwell.
The town is founded, and is founded well.
Not Cecrops, who with Athens' deathless fame
Has, as its founder, linked his honored name;
Nor Romulus, who with proud Rome must blend
His fame and glory till the world shall end,
Had more of courage and subduing toil,
Or reaped a richer harvest from the soil.
Austin and Kinsman each had built a town,
Called by their names, and fraught with wide renown.
And Smith, in Vernon, had a fame acquired,
As one who settled in a place retired.
And other towns, of which far less I knew,
Were rising up, like new-born Isles, to view.
Their deeds, in prose, on some bright page shall glow,
Or, in soft numbers, shall hereafter flow.
To these old settlements our founders sped
For earthly comfort and for heavenly bread.
A mill and meeting there they joy to find—
Food for the body, and th' immortal mind.

The white man comes—the red man hastes away
No bark canoes on Pymatuning play;
Their council fires along its shores grow dim;
To savage strains succeeds the gospel hymn.

Look once again! Another house behold!
Not made of marble, nor o'erlaid with gold;
It has no lofty spire, no sounding bell,
Whose tones with all-commanding accents swell.
In its broad aisle no Brussels carpet lies,
Nor furnace range the wintry cold defies.
Yet godly men and women gather there
To hear of Jesus, and unite in prayer.
When no ambassador their worship leads,
Some charming reader Davis' Sermons reads,
To hear a Jones or Andrews reading there,
Is a high privilege I joy to share.
In sacred songs their thanks to God they raise;
In good old tunes they offer up their praise.
By Captain Leonard now the choir is led,
Or Elisha Giddings e'er with music fed.
Mear or St. Martin's now I hear them name,
Or else Old Hundred, with its world-wide fame.
How many, who there sweetly sang, have gone,
In higher notes and purer strains, to join!
Celestial music in their anthems flow,
And their sweet tones to heaven's vast concave go!
They have a settled pastor—all draw near—
'Tis E. T. Woodruff—name to me e'er dear.
To a large Church the bread of life he breaks,
And for their welfare prayer on prayer he makes.

If living, let his sun in peace go down,
And stars of splendor gem his future crown,
His eldest deacon rises to my gaze
Like to some patriarch of older days:
Like unto Moses when he held the rod,
Or like to Enoch when he walked with God.
The name of Ezra Leonard need be told
To only those who saw him not of old.
He dies, but lo! his mantle falls
On those who take his place on Zion's walls.
While these things rise within this house of prayer.
Men of another creed a house prepare—
Men to whose hearts the name of Wesley's dear
And who the things he taught they still revere.
Among the preachers whom I there behold,
The names of Morse and Carr must first be told.
An Elliott and a Snasey once there taught,
And to make known the means of pardon sought.
And while I gaze, temples on temples rise,
With spires and turrets pointing to the skies,
In beauteous form on every street they stand,
And incense to the God of heaven demand.
Where ravens croaked, we hear the Sabbath bell,
And songs that to the sounding archways swell.
Who stays at home to sleep God's holy day
Has no excuse; a church stands o'er the way.
I look again, and on my tearful eyes
The graveyards of those early days arise.
I see them all. But one wakes in my soul
Emotions deep, defying all control,
My eldest sister sleeps in quiet there;
My parents in those dreamless slumbers share!
My brothers, children, there are laid away
To rest, till the great resurrection day.
Within those vaults where mortal labors close,
How many fair and lovely ones repose!
There many a cherished daughter sleeps,
While o'er her urn the lonely mother weeps.
How many a wife, snatched from affections arms,
And blest by God with most endearing charms,
In melting tones proclaims the sad farewell,
And in these silent mansions comes to dwell.
How many a lover, when about to come
And take possession of some happy home,
With feelings undescribed her hopes gives o'er,
She enters here, and meets her friends no more.
Thus, dearest friends, of life in every stage,
From smiling infants up to hoary age,
Are in these narrow cells with sadness laid,
In beauteous forms of earth no more arrayed.
How many funeral trains, by Palmer led,
Are drawing near those cities of the dead.

Solemn and slow, they move, they pass along,
All is impressive—he controls the throng.
But from these mournful scenes we now must turn,
We leave the tombstone and the mouldering urn,
While bridal halls, with glowing lights appear,
And youth and beauty, clad in white draw near,
They, at the nuptial altar graceful stand,
To make their vows, and join in heart and hand.
In fifty years what joyous circles meet—
What bridegrooms, and what smiling brides we greet.
In later days, in climes from Wayne afar,
I've seen those circles gemmed by many a star;
But in my mind no thoughts so deep are driven,
As where *E. C. is to †S. W. given.
There is a generous invitation, large and wide,
And Harvey Coe, does o'er the scene preside.
The miry roads, the clouds, cannot control
The beaming, joyous sunshine of the soul.

Like diamonds sparkling in a golden crown,
The schools of Wayne are worthy their renown.
Her teachers like the sages of the past,
Lay broad foundations, which through time shall last.
To print their names in lines of light and gold,
And to the world their humble toils unfold,
Is a fond tribute I would gladly give;
But on a brighter page their names shall live.
Amid the earliest of that faithful band,
I see my loved (now sainted) mother stand.
When Wayne is but a prattling infant child,
She rocks its cradle 'mid the forests wild,
Like one who throws a pebble from the shore,
She starts a wave which rolls for evermore.

Amid the buildings on Wayne's faithful ground
I look in vain for one; 'twill not be found:
No shop for selling liquid death I see,
Where men are murdered for a trifling fee.
A shop like this she never did sustain,
And in its absence, there's eternal gain.
Her fields are greener, and her tents more fair,
A purer love her wives and children share,
More of her sons the Church of Christ adorn,
Or meet for worship on God's holy morn.

Of military men Wayne well might boast;
They seem like captains of King David's host.
Some, in their youth, with England did contend,
Or Western homes from savage tribes defend.

---
*Eliza Coleman.   †Sylvester Ward.

Her Colonels, and her Generals form so vast array,
I cannot take them in at one survey.
In civil officers she puts implicit trust,
Her justices ('tis thought) have all been just,
Her judge fills up the measure of his fame,
He dies—Judge Hayes—but we revere his name.
Jones and Bartholomew, at times I see,
Clad with a sheriff's power to take or free.
'Mid lists of chief commissioners enrolled,
Are names of Tuttles, honored e'er of old.
She has physicians, learned and skilled to heal ;
Allen and Hotchkiss the first years reveal,
Spellman and others of a later day ;
They, by God's aid, restrict diseases sway.
She has a statesman of surpassing fame ;
His deeds in Congress give to him a name.
When he for freedom speaks, the echoes fall
On despot's thrones, and every Bastile wall ;
The dungeons of the slave with gladness ring,
While proud oppressors quake like Babylon's king
Upon that fearful night, that dreadful day,
When sceptre, crown and life, all passed away.
In Congress let a Gidding's voice be heard,
Till for the slave all sympathies are stirred,
And freedom down our nation's streets shall roll
Like streams refreshing to the deathless soul.
But I must stop, for I no more can say,
Others must speak on this eventful day,
From Plymouth Rock I send this greeting home :
"My heart is with you, though I cannot come."
In all my walks and wanderings here I trace
The well-known foot-prints of a giant race.
The pilgrim fathers sure were men of God ;
They sought his glory when these wilds they trod,
If their descendants in their footsteps go,
Then streams of bliss in deep'ning tides shall flow.
Millennial banners soon shall be unfurled,
And one glad anthem fill a radiant world.

THE
Seventy-Fifth Anniversary,

August 24th, 1878.

PRELIMINARY PROCEEDINGS.

During the season of 1878, a frequent topic of conversation between the aged and those in middle life, was, in regard to the propriety of celebrating the Seventy-Fifth Anniversary of the Settlement of our Township, as a connecting link between the past, present and future; no move, however, was made in that direction, until about the last days of July, when an article appeared in the *Ashtabula Sentinel*, from the Wayne correspondent, calling the attention of our citizens to the matter, to the near approach of the proper day, and showing how many of the Officers and Committees of the Semi-Centennial were still living, and that probably few, if any, would be living to attend the Centennial Meeting of 1903, and urging the importance of celebrating this the *Seventy-Fifth* anniversary.

August 4th, the following notice was read from the several pulpits.

"All who are interested in celebrating the Seventy-Fifth Anniversary of the settlement of Wayne Township, are requested to meet in the Congregational Church, on Monday (to-morrow) evening, to consider the matter, and make the necessary arrangements."

A goodly number of enthusiastic people gathered. Mr. WOLCOTT MINER was elected temporary chairman, and Mr. S. A. BABCOCK secretary.

After remarks upon the importance of the Anniversary, by Mr. L. H. Jones and others, it was

RESOLVED, That we celebrate such Anniversary on the 24th day of August, 1878.

Going into permanent organization, the following Officers and Committees, who served, were selected:

President..................F. E. JONES.
Vice Presidents...........D. L. ROBERTS, E. A. FOBES, H. S. SIMPKINS.
Secretaries................S. A. BABCOCK, R. M. JONES.
Treasurer..................WM. B. SMILIE.
Marshals...................J. B. NOXON, S. JONES, JR., J. B. WILCOX.
Chaplain...................REV. D. WOODWORTH.
Com. on Speakers..........S. JONES, JR., D. SMILIE; J. W. GRAHAM.
Com. on Entertainment...R. M. JONES AND WIFE, W. MINER AND WIFE, H. S. SIMPKINS AND WIFE, WM. B. SMILIE AND WIFE, J. B. NOXEN AND WIFE, A. J. HATCH AND WIFE, B. E. McGRANAHAN AND WIFE, E. D. WARD AND WIFE, C. B. HAYES AND WIFE, WM. E. CAMP AND WIFE, F. E. JONES AND WIFE, MILO WILCOX AND WIFE, C. WILDER AND WIFE, M. E. FOBES AND WIFE, P. A. WARD AND WIFE, MISS C. E. BABCOCK, MISS MIRIAM WALWORTH, MISS DORCAS FONNER, MISS CARRIE COLEMAN, CASPER MONTGOMERY, ALEX. BROWN.
Com. on Music.............H. S. SIMPKINS, E. T. WILCOX, S. JONES, JR.
Com. on Ancient Music...L. H. JONES, A. J. GIDDINGS, N. WILCOX.
Com. on preparing a place of meeting.....} O. H. MINER, WILL WARD, S. W. BAILEY, W. F. PELTON, C. B. HAYES, ALEX. BROWN, H. PEASE, GEORGE HART, O. H. P. WING, T. BATTRICK.

Com. on Finance............W. E. JONES, L. L. FOBES, M. F. DEAN.

Com. on Decorations......F. A. KINNEAR, MRS. T. BATTRICK, MRS. M. F. DEAN, MISSES MIRIAM WALWORTH, SARAH BATTRICK, CARRIE COLEMAN.

Com. on Invitations from abroad......... } CAP. R. L. JONES, S. P. FOBES, R. HAYES.

Com. on old Relics.........O. H. MINER, D. HART, S. P. FOBES, M. F. DEAN.

Historian..................L. H. JONES.

Chiefs of Police............CONSTABLES L. H. FOBES, S. E. FOSTER.

Assistant Police............FRANK WARD, CASPER MONTGOMERY, E. H. JONES, J. B. WILCOX, ANDREW SHARP, N. LEONARD, HENRY CROUCH, GEORGE MARVIN.

Only three weeks intervened between the decision to celebrate and the set day, and all was bustle and excitement; but the arrival of the day found our people ready. The morning dawned beautiful, and it remained so throughout the day; the clouds of dust upon the roads rendered travel unpleasant, but the beautiful cool and shady woods was all the more inviting.

The Committee was fortunate in securing of Mr. O. H. Miner, the same beautiful grove in which the Semi-Centennial Anniversary was held, twenty-five years ago. The grounds were seated for one thousand persons.

THE STAGE

about 15x36 feet, was raised three feet from the ground. Tables for the Secretaries and Press were placed in convenient positions. Chairs and settees were provided for the old people, Ancient Choir and speakers. A rustic railing ran along in front, made of limbs of trees and grape vines. The speakers' stand was a plain board supported by forked saplings for legs.

At the rear of the stand, on a board, was "1803" very tastefully formed with heads of wheat, then the word "Welcome," and on still another board, in immortelles, "1878."

The stage was profusely decorated with flowers, and directly in front of the speakers' table was a pyramid formed of moss and flowers, on the face of which was "1803—1878," in immortelles.

Various mottoes were placed upon the trees, such as "The Past Gone," "The Present Here," "Peace," "Happiness," "Prosperity," etc.; also numerous beautiful pictures, which contributed not a little to the general make up.

Upon the stand were arranged for exhibition numerous

ANCIENT RELICS.

Miss Cloe Fobes, now of Kinsman, contributed three pewter platters, 145 years old, once the property of Abiel Jones; a red cloak, 140 years old, and a black dress, 75 years old, formerly owned by Mrs. Elizabeth Fobes; a brown dress, 75 years old, formerly owned and worn by Betsy Darrow ; and a dainty pair of slippers, 100 years old, that Mrs. Bethiah Fobes once wore.

Mr. S. P. Fobes exhibited a musket and powder-horn, 134 years old, formerly the property of A. Huntley ; a knee buckle, 90 years old ; and a sword, carried by Capt. Simon Fobes through the Revolutionary war.

Mr. O. H. Miner exhibited a brass warming pan, that has descended to him through four generations. His daughter, Miss Elizabeth, exhibited a teacup, saucer and spoon, of great age, once the property of her great-great-grand-mother, Mrs. Joel Miner.

Mr. R. M. Jones exhibited a handsome chair, 150 years old, once the property of Capt. Alpheus Billings. It was brought from Connecticut by Joseph B. Barber.

L. H. Foster exhibited a hand-saw, 150 years old.

A bible, printed by the American Bible Society, in 1818, and purchased soon after by Rev. H. A. Babcock, was exhibited by his son, S. A. Babcock.

There were also the

RECORDS OF WAYNE

township, since its organization. The preface reads :

Record of the township of Wayne, in the County of Ashtabula and State of Ohio, instituted by the constituted authority of the County of Trumbull, in the last moments of her jurisdiction over said tract now known by the appropriate name of Wayne, and after it was annexed to the County of Ashtabula, as doth appear from page second.

There were also the poll books of Wayne, from 1811, forward ; also a record of ear-marks, something curious to the people of to-day. As a sample of an ear-mark record, we publish one :

WAYNE, July 13th, 1811.
Then recorded for Nathan Fobes, ear-mark, a slit in the left ear. Recorded by me.

NATHANIEL COLEMAN,
T. Clerk.

A bush hook, two sickles and various early implements completed the exhibit.

A steady stream of happy people poured in upon the scene to the number of about two thousand, among them Earl Daniels' Martial Band, and the Gustavus and Orangeville Cornet Bands.

Among the old people, escorted to a seat upon the stand, were Mr. Samuel Jones, Sr., and Mrs. Rosannah Lowery. The former in his ninety eighth year, is very deaf, but was exceedingly happy to be present; the latter was ninety one in June, 1878. She settled in Trumbull (Co.) the same year that Capt. Joshua Fobes came to Wayne.

Elias Fobes, the boy who lived in this township the *first winter* of 1803-4, is still living, in Williamsfield, but was unable to be present.

After a general hand-shake, and the renewal of old acquaintances, etc., the President, Mr. F. E. JONES, called the meeting to order, and the Gustavus Cornet Band played a fine pieee of music; followed by Earl Daniels' Martial Band.

The Rev. Father VELORUS LAKE then read from the same ancient Bible,* the same passages of scripture that were read by Rev. GEORGE ROBERTS, (now deceased,) at the Semi-Centennial meeting.

The reading of the scriptures was followed by an appropriate prayer, by the Chaplain, Rev. DARIUS WOODWORTH.

REMARKS OF THE PRESIDENT.

The President then addressed the assembly in a few well chosen words, stating that the object of the meeting was to " revive the histories of the past, rivet them upon the present, and hand them down to the future; to renew old acquaintances, shake the hands of old friends, to look once more into their faces; to grow younger, happier and better. Many of those who helped to settle and found this township lived to join in the Semi-Centennial Anniversary, but

---

*See page 6.

they are nearly all gone now. Those who were in the active walks of life twenty-five years ago, and who formed the officers and committees of that day, are, if living, among the old people of to-day; twenty-five years hence, when the Centennial will be celebrated, most, if not all of them, will be gone; hence the importance of this meeting as a connecting link of the past with the future.

We welcome you, fellow citizens and friends, from whatever clime, of whatever race, to the joys and festivities of this day."

The President then called upon one of the Secretaries to read the names of the officers and committees of the Semi-Centennial, and asked each one present to rise up as their names were called. Of those present twenty-five years ago, the following were in the assembly, and as their names were called they arose:

President—C. C. Wick.
Vice Presidents—Linus H. Jones, J. Fobes, Jr.
Secretary—Charles Fitch.
Marshal—Richard Hayes.
Assistant Marshals—Lorenzo D. Gillett, Horace F. Giddings, Chester Oatman, Lucius Gillett, S. Jones, Jr., David Hart.
Speaker—Rev. E. B. Chamberlain.
Committee on Entertainment—Anson Jones, David Parker, N. Coleman, Jr., Morris Spellman.
Committee to prepare a place of meeting—Wm. Coleman.
Committee on Finance—Simon P. Fobes.

Quite a number of the above persons served on two or three different committees. Every person now living, who served on committees twenty-five years ago, were present, except O. R. Ward, Elon Hart and G. C. Holt. The two former live in the township, but were detained on account of sickness, the former of himself, (died March 22nd, 1879,) the latter, of a friend. Mr. Holt failed to come. Then *all* who were present at that meeting were requested to rise; about one hundred responded.

THE ANCIENT CHOIR

then sang *Old Coronation.*

"All Hail the power of Jesus' name."

The Choir was led by Uncle Linus H. Jones, and consisted of the following persons:

Mrs. Rosetta McMichael, Miss Christine Noxon, Mrs. J. C. Andrews, Mrs. Leroy Hayes, Mrs. Milo Wilder, Mrs. Samuel Hubler, Mrs. A. J. Giddings, Mrs. Lydia Bearss, Mrs. S. P. Fobes, Mrs. Henry P. Wilder, Mrs. Augustus Ward, Mrs. Horace Wilcox, Mrs. Abram Griffin, Mrs. L. H. Foster, Mrs. J. B. Barber, Mrs. Plinny Case, Mrs. Elizabeth Thompson, Mrs. Horatio Woodworth, Mrs. Elon Parker, Messrs. Josiah Walker, Cyril Woodworth, Horatio Woodworth, and A. J. Giddings.

None of the old pitch-pipes having survived the changes of time, Mr. David Hart, who used to make them forty years ago, made one which did excellent service in pitching the tunes.

The President then introduced the Rev. E. B. Chamberlain, one of the speakers of twenty-five years ago, who addressed the assembly, as follows:

ADDRESS

—OF—

REV. E. B. CHAMBERLAIN.

MR. PRESIDENT, LADIES AND GENTLEMEN :—We stand to-day face to face with the conquering imperious power of *time*. We stand where we stood at the Semi-Centennial twenty-five years ago. "The same soil is beneath our feet, the same heavens are over our heads," but all else, how changed! How few that were in that assembly are here to-day. Those that were aged have crossed the river, many that were young and middle aged have passed away. The speakers who took a lively part in the proceedings of that meeting, are nearly all gone. But the recollection is too tender and pathetic to dwell upon. There is a sacred and deep feeling which silence only befits, and we stand uncovered with profound veneration in the memory of their lives and virtues. They speak to us to-day. The voiceless eloquence of one true life has no compeer among all the clamorous and pretentious voices of earth. The silence of Jesus was often more profound than the grace that flowed from his lips. The place to us seems holy, and if we speak with reluctance, it is because no sandaled foot should tread in the presence of this invisible Shekinah, no eyes unanointed, should peer between the parting folds of that rending veil of time, no lips untouched with fire from God's Altar, should speak with thoughtless air.

The first half of the century was quite fully canvassed twenty-five years ago. It is in place now, only to speak of the last twenty-five years and compare and contrast what has transpired. The history of a quarter of a century is no inconsiderable portion of our brief life. An outline is all that can be given, and the unwritten is the kernel, the written is but the husk or shell. The perfect history of no human life has yet been given, and will not be till comes that day of days, that reckoning of reckonings, that judgment of judgments, when the full life shall be revealed. There are virtues that will not be known till then, there are vices that will not be known till that review shall reveal them. Volumes might be written and not bring to light the most charming excellences of a community. God has a way of developing excellence and glory from everything. The rays of the sun fall upon a plate of pure gold and the reflection dazzles the eye; the same rays fall upon a cluster of diamonds and a mixed and compound glory is revealed; the same rays fall upon the cold and unpromising earth and the sustenance of life appears, with fragrant flowers that rival gold and are worn upon the bosom, that out-rival Solomon in all his glory. We need not try to purify rain water, the electricity and thunder of the clouds have clarified it; we need not paint a rose to make it more beautiful. If we should dot or stripe a native born lily, nature would look upon the rude daubing and laugh us to scorn. So if we try to transcribe those comely virtues that grow from industry, mental culture and the christian faith, we daub like nature's journeymen.

We turn to some of those events that are more properly subjects of remark. When we gathered here in 1853 the nation was outwardly at peace; for almost fifty years there had been nothing like war; the future was overhung with the rainbow of promise; never did human hopes rise higher, never did waving harvest invite the sickle more, never did heaven's propitious smile seem to fall on a people more. We knew not, that in the dark secrets of coming time, lay concealed the horrors of civil war. A mental strife had long been burning, thoughtful minds clearly saw that liberty and slavery could not always exist together on this soil. The leading minds of the American people were then struggling through throes of mortal agony, hoping to avert the dire calamity. Good men devoutly prayed, "Press not to our unwilling lips the bitter chalice of such a cup, as to be compelled to crush in the deadly strife, those who are bone of our bone and flesh of our flesh," or in the language of our lamented Lincoln, "that the better angels of our nature might prevail."

The war came, the calamity is remembered, few families escaped the influence òf its burning curse. Wayne and this whole region suffered their full share in the results.

It is well that a kind providence has so ordered, that the deepest heartfelt wounds may be healed by time, or alleviated by christian fortitude. The brave men who suffered are remembered with undying gratitude. The gentle rains of fourteen summers have slowly leveled down the mounds over their graves, the grass grows with luxuriance around the place, the myrtle vine creeps stealthily and slowly over their tombs, expanding its leaves and lengthening its vines, the birds in the branches of the trees above them sing as merrily as if nothing had happened. So all nature seems striving to obliterate and conceal; as Shem and Japheth walked backward with broad mantle to conceal a forbidding sight; all nature walks backward with its over-shadowing mantle, to hide the enormity from our eyes, and, as if struggling to conceal the enormity of such dreadful crimes from the eye of a compassionate but insulted God.

As to the *future* we hope, and that most kind susceptibility of the mind, *hope*, is a friend to mortals. But let us for. a few moments contemplate some of the elements of weakness attached to the Government.

First, the real cause of emancipation and enfranchisement of exslaves is a source of weakness. A desperate effort was made to save the Government as it was, with slavery untouched. Every person knows that, as a Governmental act, it was prompted not by a sense of *justice*, but as a *necessity* in the case. Compare the act with that of the Russian Government which lies but a little back in the memory of most of you, when the young Czar ascended the throne, a model man, well read, well traveled, with a clean mind, with humane impulses, he felt the pulse of the nineteenth Century, he notified the nobles and people of the empire, that he should abolish slavery or serfdom, the most iron-bound system on earth; the serfs were attached to the soil and sold with the estates. Conventions of nobles remonstrated, but nothing could move this true man from his purpose. It was not four millions, as in our case, but forty millions, and without the shedding a drop of blood or the expense of a dollar, with a dash of this noble man's pen the forty millions were freed. I ask a reflecting people what gives to that princely power its ornate beauty and strength to-day? The answer is simply that people are bound to the Government by the strongest bond that can be conceived of justice, done by force of humane and righteous feelings. We may be sure the colored people will remember the toil, sacrifice, earnest philanthropic and christian effort, that for long years was made for their emancipation, but they were released only by the necessities of war! They thank the Government, as we thank a tornado that leveled for us a wall we could not climb. The moral force of the act is not an element of strength, but weakness.

Again, unlimited enfranchisement with no condition but that of age, is an element of weakness. Do not understand the speaker as wishing to criticize our form of Government, but if we would be strong, we must know our weakness. Every man in America has a king's heart beating under his side, and every woman with more than queenly dignity, rules in the good or evil in the country. Intelligence, a clear knowledge of the rights and duties of the citizen, and a willingness at all times to vote and take the responsibilities of a citizen are requisite. If it were required that a voter should hold a certain amount of property, or that he should be able to read the constitution and laws of the land, it might be safer. But when a farmer, mechanic or merchant, by care, industry and hard labor, has his vote neutralized by an indolent and irresponsible man who owns nothing, he is liable to have his interests voted away, to be taxed to the verge of endurance, with no remedy or protection. The genius of our Government welcomes all of foreign birth and we would not have it otherwise. We remember that Benedict Arnold was an American, and that La Fayette, a most noble French philanthropist in the days of the Revolution was a true friend, and thus, to a great extent it is now; but to naturalize foreigners by thousands, who have no knowledge of our constitution and laws, and who cannot read, is weakness, and not strength.

Again, a laxity of views in the fundamental principles of morality, is an element of weakness. There can be no strength in the Government where there is a lack of private and family integrity. The history of the past is given for our instruction. Where lay the strength of Rome, when the world trembled at her mandates? It is recorded that in the zenith of her power, there was not the sundering of a marriage bond in all her wide empire, for the space of 170 years. There was no battle cry that came to the Roman heart like that, "For the altar and the hearth." The whole fabric of the commonwealth rose out of the family. To a great extent this was true of the early American history. The growing looseness of the times is an element of weakness. Defalcation, dishonesty in those who are entrusted with public funds is weakening, or is an element of weakness which must be apparent to all. "Whom can we trust?" is now the question, and it needs no prophet to foretell the failure of popular Government, if private and public character is so perverse. The elements of weakness are many and threatening enough to make the next quarter of the century look dark and forbidding; but it is not our wisdom to be discouraged by these things. Another war may come. May a merciful Heaven forbid! Look at the claims now before Congress, amounting to three hundred and twenty millions of dollars for property in the Southern States, destroyed by the progress of the war.

But there are elements of strength in the times and in the Government, that bid us all take heart and hope. The enemy of free Government can no longer taunt us, as did England's sarcastic poet, with

"The fustian flag that proudly waves,
In mockery o'er a land of slaves."

That flag has been regenerated and baptized in blood. It is a more sacred Ægis, it has a deeper meaning than ever it had before, as redemption is more sacred by the blood of the cross, human liberty is more valued by the sacrifice that maintains it. The "Grand army of the Republic," will not sleep, the good people of the country see with eyes unscaled, and are jealous with a patriotic jealousy; the past twenty-five years is a teacher and preacher, bitter the lesson, but lasting the result, the living and the dead cry out. The voice of millions of the living will cry *beware* at the first presumptuous step. Six hundred thousand noble men who perished in the calamity of that war, now raise their snowy hands from the margin of the spirit shore, crying, "God palsy the arm that is stretched forth to pluck one stone from the fair temple of American justice and freedom!" That flag so much praised as "sacred, pure, unsullied, lofty," in our infant ears, that in our childish fancy we thought must be a scrap cut by the soft hands of angels, from the curtain of the ether blue, with the stars all in it. Men and brethren, it belongs to the coming twenty-five years to determine whether this Government shall stand and answer the expectation of its illustrious founders, or whether the grand experiment shall fail; pardon the supposition even of a failure. If this generation shall be wise and virtuous, faithful to God and humanity, that flag will ever wave, and when the sun shall pale and the moon turn to blood, when the earth shall reel and stagger like a drunken man, the last man on its trembling surface may see the flag of American liberty waving. Go down it may; go down it must; go down it will; but it will go down only with the wreck of matter and the final crash of worlds! May a merciful Heaven save us in the plentitude of divine grace, and "violence no more be heard in our land."

Respected and dear friends, it is a source of unqualified satisfaction to me, to meet with you on this occasion. We all have an important part to act for this life, and a vastly more important one to act for the life to come. We cannot trust ourselves to speak freely of former associations. The youth of our labors was spent in this and Trumbull County. Many of you we have baptized in the name of the sacred Trinity. In twelve townships there are living very many that we have united in the sacred bonds of marriage. In hundreds of families we have endeavored to comfort the afflicted, and performed the last funeral rites of over seven hundred friends, and in weakness, fear and much trembling, have tried to point you all to the Lamb of God.

We have spoken of the departed; they are embalmed and treasured in our memory. We do not forget that your feet and mine will, erelong, wearied and worn, be treading the margin of that river of death. We love and cleave to the present life, but there is a better life to come, if we are faithful.

"These earthly homes are fair and bright,
  Tho' clouds will sometimes come;
But oh, we long to see the light,
  That gilds our Heavenly home."

May we say to the young, bear in mind that parents live for their children, and one generation lives for another. The early settlers of this place came here, not for themselves alone; they came for you, they toiled and suffered and sacrificed for you; they did not wish you to be ever dwelling upon the fact of their anxiety for you. If you have ever erred and wandered, you cannot know the deep solicitude and deathless love they have felt, even as

> "None of the ransomed ever knew
> How deep were the waters crossed,
> Or how dark was the night the Lord passed through,
> Ere he found his sheep that was lost."

You have abundant reason to take pride in the just principles and christian faith of your noble ancestors; with such a vantage ground as you stand upon, an obligation rests upon you to make advancements in all that is good, enterprising and noble; "Other men labored and ye are entered into their labors."

Aged friends, there is *rest* by and by. Rest is a lawful craving of the weary soul; the jaded ploughman loves lengthened shadows. There is a diamond of eloquence in that scripture, "There the weary be at rest." That is not inaction; Jesus did not say come to death for rest, or come to the *grave* for rest, but "Come unto me for rest." The lake or river bound in a prison of ice, does not suggest repose, but the gently moving stream, full, deep and clear, fills all the chambers of the soul with calm repose. The clouds covering all, give not the feeling of rest, but when the light clouds chase each other across the back-ground of a clear blue sky, the feeling is of serene repose—"God rested." Oh, think of the movement of the starry worlds on high, as in grandeur and eternal harmony they move, and then think of that sublime announcement in Genesis, "God rested;" magnificent and glorious rest of God! This is the rest that the Saviour calls us to. There is a sense in which the grave is a rest, but the rest that remains for the people of God is not the damp chambers of the tomb.

There is a *home*. We are strangers here, but are going home. The love of home is one of the first-born passions of the human breast; little children build play houses, and larger children construct mansions and stake out lands, which we sometimes too fondly call our own. This natural longing will be gratified; the house not made with hands is a spiritual house, its foundations are laid deep in the grace of God, and every lively stone in the vast superstructure is laid on with grace, and erelong the topmost stone will be laid with shoutings of grace, grace unto it, with its exalted and burnished dome, streaked with light from Heaven's own throne; O Christian, that is your home!

The present gathering is a called meeting, the regular appointment is, by the adjournment of a former meeting, "to meet August 24th, at the Centre Church, at 10 o'clock a. m., 1903, and when you adjourn this meeting, it will be simply taking a recess for twenty-five years. The people of Wayne have large farms, large hearts, large ideas and large aspirations. Most people think that they do well to keep up with the times, but it seems that you are prone to go in advance of the times. It is fortunate that you called this meeting; many would otherwise fail to receive the wholesome satisfaction that is now given to us. It is truly a joyful day; the sun in the heavens smiles in all his beauty, the taste here displayed in the decoration of the grounds, the wealth of mottos of flowers, of thoughtful preparation for the comfort and convenience of guests, the relics of ancient times, the joyful faces and warm greetings which here meet us are indeed a benediction long to be cherished, and held in grateful remembrance through the remnant of life.

The men and women that we called old twenty-five years ago are all gone, with only here and there an exception; would that we could do or say something to cheer and comfort them on the borders of time; but, if we cannot do that, may we not receive, with full and thankful hearts, the opulent wealth of their kind and prayerful benediction.

In conclusion, allow me to say to the people of Wayne, in behalf of all other guests, as well as ourselves, we present to you our most cordial and heartfelt thanks, that you have granted us this distinguished favor to be present to-day. Distance will separate us in body; but in spirit we shall be with you, joying and rejoicing in your continued prosperity.

After the close of Mr. Chamberlain's address, a part of the Wayne choir sang

"O, be Joyful in God."

The names of the singers were as follows: *Leader*, Wm. B. Smilie; *Organist*, Mrs. Lottie Jones; *Soprano*, Mrs. Lottie Jones, Miss Carrie Gillett, Mrs. Wm. B. Smilie; *Alto*, Mrs. Jennie McNeilly, Mrs. Hattie McGranahan; *Bass*, Wm. B. Smilie, Lucius L. Fobes, Philo B. McNeilly; *Tenor*, B. E. McGranahan, E. T. Wilcox, Orlando Woodworth.

We were happy to have with us our old President of twenty-five years ago, Calvin C. Wick, now of Ashland, O., who was next introduced, and as his towering form and gray head arose to come forward, he was greeted with a subdued though hearty round of applause, such as was befitting to one of his years.

MR. WICK'S REMARKS.

He said, "My friends, you cannot realize my embarrassment in coming before you. I did not expect to come, but your committee almost commanded me to come. Seventy-five years ago the first white settler came here to this unbroken forest; to-day, what a change. Forty-eight years ago a boy came trudging along your streets, not to settle here but just for a time; but he stayed, many long years—the best of his life, and became ingrafted as one of you; to-day he stands before you.

I knew most of the early settlers, their trials and perseverance. Where are they to-day? I visited the grave-yard where they lie, my friends, and it seemed to me as I looked at the head-stones, that they all lie there, but as I look over this vast assembly, and as I have been permitted to shake your hands, I see yet among you many familiar faces. But there are many strangers. Then there are the young, in whose faces are the family resemblance; and I am glad to see in the present generation, so many earnest sons and daughters of their noble ancestors. May heaven bless you, may you go on ever standing firm to maintain the solid principles laid down by your fathers and mothers."

His remarks were frequently broken with emotion, and the tears often streamed down his cheeks, as he attempted to tell of the bygone days.

As we looked into his face and that of Rev. Mr. Chamberlain, and heard their voices once more, we felt well paid for all our efforts in this anniversary; had they failed to come, one-half of its interest would have been lost.

After music by Orangeville Band, which arrived about that time, Mr. S. A. Babcock read the following poem:

NAMING OF WILLIAMSFIELD.*

In days of yore (as tales relate,)
Old Wayne selects a country seat
Along the pleasant fertile plains,
Contiguous to the State of Penn.

Sir William was his darling child,
Who, with his father seeks the wild,
And with assidious strength of arm,
Assists his sire to clear the farm.

The eastern part had upland soil,
That well might pay the laborers' toil;
The West had meadows fair and green,
And Pymatuning rolled between.

Paternal love and filial care,
Unite each toilsome hour to cheer,
And hope's bright sunbeams seemed to play
More gaily each succeeding day;

While north and south and east and west,
Acknowledge them supremely blest.
Their fields the golden harvest bear,
And yield them sweet and wholesome fare.

The farm was large—the sire proposed
While he the western part enclosed,
Tilled by his son the east should yield,
And thence they called it WILLIAM'S-FIELD.

---

*This Poem on the division of Wayne and Williamsfield, was written by Miss Evelina Babcock, about forty-seven years ago. It was printed in the papers of that day, causing much unsuccessful conjecture as to who was its author.

Thus days passed on, and months and years,
Unpressed by cares unchilled by fears;
The numerous progeny they rear,
Like Jacob's goodly tents appear.

At length the sire addressed the son,
"Till now our farm has been but one,
Our children now will want their shares.
Let us divide it with our heirs."

"Agreed," says William "show the line,
How much is yours, how much is mine?"
"The eastern part by tilling well,
Will give your children place to dwell."

The sons of William then arose,
With haughty voice they thus oppose,
"Mark your broad stream and meadows fair,
Be that our line, we'll meet you there."

At this the father shook his head,
Yet seemed composed, then calmly said,
"One-half the farm you've long possessed,
My other son must have the rest."

The sons then rose with dauntless air,
And said, "no more this name we'll bear,
We'll be a race distinct and free,
Hence severed be our unity."

THE DINNER.

This completed the forenoon's programme, and the Marshals formed the procession and marched to dinner as follows:

1. BANDS.
2. SPEAKERS.
3. EDITORS.
4. ANCIENT CHOIR.
5. INVITED GUESTS.
6. PIONEER CITIZENS.

Of the dinner, the Editor of the *Sentinel* wrote as follows:
"When dinner was announced, the procession marched under an arch, over which was in large letters "WELCOME." Under majestic maples we found four tables laid with clean white cloth, and as carefully spread with dishes as you would find at a hotel. These tables in this grand dining room measured 206 feet, forming a square, in the centre of which was a long table loaded with provisions. Two cook stoves were boiling the best coffee we ever drank at any gathering, and vastly better than nine-tenths of hotel coffee. There were a great many beautiful cakes; one pyramidical one had this question on it: "Will you be here in 1903?" Well, for ourselves we say we will try, if the same cook makes the cake.

The tables were filled with hungry people, and after an impressive asking of a blessing by Rev. Mr. Chamberlain, were served by ladies and gentlemen, as quietly and with no more confusion than by so many trained waiters."

The Editor of the *Gazette* wrote as follows:
"No hotel could have served a dinner better, or served a better dinner. There were pyramid cakes, jelly cakes, pies, frosted cakes of various kinds, cold meats, delicious biscuits, rich golden butter, and coffee; well, it makes one's mouth water to think of all the good things. Our great regret now is that we could not eat more; but there was a hungry editor at our right and a nice old lady at our left, and we gauged our appetite by the length of time it took them to eat."

AN AMUSING INCIDENT.

Just at the close of dinner, Mr. S. E. Foster, one of the chief of Police, dressed in full Indian costume, with feathers in his hair, mounted on a black charger, came dashing from the woods into the grove, uttering at the same time wild war whoops, causing as much consternation for a moment as if a real Massassauger had suddenly risen from his long resting place and come once more to demand fire-water or something else, as he was wont to do of our ancestors seventy-five years ago.

AFTERNOON.

After the bountiful dinner and more hand-shaking, the assembly was called to order by Vice President E. A. Fobes, and the three bands alternated in furnishing us with an abundance of excellent music. The bands were composed of the following gentlemen :

GUSTAVUS BAND.

O. E. Henry, M. D. Cowden, A. H. Goff, P. J. Morey, H. J. Barnes, Perry Cooper, Frank Banning, H. T. Waters, P. S. Supplee, D. L. Sheldon, A. P. Case, J. B. Shipman, F. F. Shipman.

ORANGEVILLE BAND.

A. Moffett, G. E. Thompson, Carl Moffett, John Thompson, E. D. Hyde, C. A. Carmer, Scott McFarland, Walter McFarland, T. Wheeler, Frank Turner, Fred Hopkins, Aaron Richards, Fred Mattox.

DANIELS' MARTIAL BAND.

James Davis, Fifer; Earl Daniels, Snare Drum; Robert King, Bass Drum.

The President then introduced the Hon. S. A. Northway, of Jefferson, who spoke as follows:

ADDRESS

—OF—

HON. S. A. NORTHWAY.

MR. PRESIDENT, LADIES AND GENTLEMEN :—I cannot enter fully into your feelings and sympathies to-day, nor appreciate, to its fullest extent, your enthusiasm in greeting one another on this occasion. I have never been a resident of your township, nor am I connected with its inhabitants in any manner, other than as a citizen of the county. But, when I look upon this great throng before me, upon these aged people close about me, and witness your unbounded enthusiasm as you take one another by the hand in that warm, hearty clasp, which indicates a friendship that has come up through a long number of years, and has been steady, pure and devoted; when I look upon these beautiful preparations and contemplate the pleasure with which they have been made; and when I see about me so much which speaks of happy homes, I cannot but be filled with rejoicings with you, and feel a thrill of enthusiasm in being permitted to join with you on this occasion, of the Seventy-Fifth Anniversary of the settlement of your township.

Full of these feelings, and surrounded as we are by all that can make the occasion one of enjoyment, I will speak to you in a somewhat rambling manner of the past and present of your township.

And here let me remark, that I do not see what I have done, what punishment you should desire to heap upon me, in forcing me to follow the able gentleman who addressed you in the fore part of the day, and who so clearly and ably spoke to us of our past, present and future—one who has been your beloved pastor, who has helped to lay over seven hundred of your neighbors, friends and citizens of the surrounding country in the grave—one who has stood by your bedside in sickness, and your fireside in health, who has united you in the bonds of matrimony, and taken you by the hand and counseled you in the way that leads to a higher life. I say, I cannot see why I should be expected to add anything to what he has so well said.

But bear with me while I present some facts relative to the early history of your township.

Twenty-five years ago to-day you met upon this spot, and beneath this deep forest shade, to celebrate the Semi-Centennial of the settlement of this township. Then many of those who came here in 1803-4 and 5 were present, and engaged in its celebration, and helped to recount the hardships of those earlier days. Of that number, not one is here to-day. Elias Fobes, who, of all that number is the only one now alive, is too infirm to be with us. He is the only living link to bind you to the settlement of your township. He, too, will soon be gone, and then not one will be left who can speak to you of the toils incident to the settlement of your township seventy-five years ago. Yonder cemetery has kindly gathered all into its embrace. But, though dead, they are not forgotten, nor has their influence ceased. They live in almost everything about us; in the broad and smiling fields, blooming with the golden harvest; in the pleasant homes around us, where happiness is enthroned in the family; in the schools and churches whose foundations they laid; in the pure, moral and religious principles which they made the chief corner-stone of all their undertakings, and whose influence is so clearly manifest in your community to-day.

It may not be improper for me to advert to some of the early incidents of our county, as well as of your township. The first settlement (if it could be called a settlement) made in this county was by one—Halstead, sometime about 1790. At least he was found here by a surveying party, in what is now the township of Conneaut, in 1796, and he claimed to have been here several years prior to that date. Very little is known of him. What brought him alone into the wilds, I am unable to state. Civilization seemed to have no charms for him, and shortly after the appearance of the surveying party he left, and I believe we have no trace of him after his going.

The first white family to spend a winter in the county, and I believe on the Reserve, was that of James Kingsbury, at Conneaut, in 1796-7.

In looking at the magnificently spread tables here to-day, we would think that starvation would be a term known only to dictionary. Yet, such is not the fact, for it actually invaded this family of Mr. Kingsbury. The father had been called back to his former home in the east, shortly after getting his family into the house, occupied by the surveying party I have before mentioned, leaving his wife and children alone in the then unbroken wilderness. He expected to be gone but a short time, but unfortunately, he was prostrated with sickness just as he was ready to start for home, and was sick for several weeks. There were no means of communicating with his family. His wife and children looked long and anxiously for him, and at length mourned him as dead. As soon as able he started for his home. At Presque Isle, he procured twenty pounds of flour, and on foot he carried it through the forest to his family. On arriving at his home, he found his wife who had been confined during his absence, so weak from actual starvation as to be unable to arise from her bed to greet him, and by her side lay her dead infant, which had died for the want of nourishment, while, but a short time before another child had also died. Thus, during his absence, his wife, who was herself nearing her end, by that most horrible of all deaths, starvation, she saw two of her children expire before her from famishing hunger.

I allude to this to show you what others suffered that we might have comfort. And when you are prone to repine at your lot and think your surroundings are poor and cheerless, just remember the hardships that were endured by those who first brought civilization to the then western wilds.

Harpersfield was settled in 1798, and the first settlers lived on corn meal, made by pounding the corn in a stump hollowed out, or upon meal or flour carried upon their backs from some point many miles away in Pennsylvania. This was the first permanent settlement made in the county of Ashtabula, the family of Mr. Kingsbury, to which I have before alluded, having left Conneaut and gone further west.

The townships of Conneaut, Austinburg, Windsor and Monroe were settled in 1799, Morgan in 1801, Geneva in 1802 and your township of Wayne in 1803.

The first house built in the county, was that built by the surveying party, in 1796, it being the one in which the Kingsbury family spent the winter of 1796-7.

The first marriage was that of Aaron Wright to Anna Montgomery, both of Conneaut, in 1800. There were no Ministers or Justices of the Peace then in Conneaut, so for the want of carriages or palace coaches to ride in, they walked through the woods, some twenty or twenty-five miles to Harpersfield, where one Wheeler, a Justice of the Peace, pronounced the ceremony that made them husband and wife.

The first child born in the county was that of James Kingsbury, of which I have before spoken, it being the one that died from starvation.

The first adult person who died in the county, was J. Gleason, in August 1798, in Harpersfield.

* The first school taught was in Harpersfield in 1802, by Elizabeth Harper, afterwards the wife of Judge Tappan.

The first Saw Mill was erected in Windsor in 1800, by Solomon Griswold, and the first Grist Mill was erected in Austinburg in 1801, by Ambrose Humphrey. All of these events transpired before Wayne was settled, and so far as we now know, before any white man, save one, had entered its borders.

Titus Hayes, then a young man, full of zeal, and fired with a love for adventure, with no companions but his ever ready gun and faithful dog, had entered the township somewhere near its northeast corner as early as 1798. His was the first tread of white man upon its soil. What his feelings were as he passed nearly over the ground we are now upon, and listened to the songs of the birds, which, for the first time since the forests were formed was poured forth upon civilized ears, we can only conjecture. He afterwards became a resident of the township, and for years, was one of the leading and most respected citizens of our community. The brave man passed to his reward more than forty-five years ago.

The first road laid out in the county, was the " Old Girdled

Road," in 1797, from Conneaut through Sheffield, Plymouth, Austinburg, Trumbull and into Geauga County.

In 1801-2, the "Old Salt Road" was opened from Ashtabula through Austinburg, Morgan, New Lyme, Wayne, Gustavus and into Kinsman. These were neither macadamized roads nor free turnpikes, except in one particular, all persons were free to pass over them as often as they could and chose to do so.

The "Old Salt Road" was so called, because the salt which was brought from New York along the Lake Shore to Ashtabula, was drawn along this marked and underbrushed way into the various townships through which the route lay. I will remark as I pass, that salt was then *very* cheap, being only about $20 per barrel.

In 1804, at the close of the year, there were, counting two bachelors for a family—I might as well stop to say, that then as now, two bachelors made a mighty small and poorly appointed family—just ninety-three families in the county, of which twenty-seven were in Harpersfield, twenty in Conneaut, seventeen in Austinburg, thirteen in Morgan or seventy-seven families in four townships.

The first mail route was established in 1803, from Warren, in Trumbull County, to Mesopotamia, Windsor, Morgan, Austinburg, Harpersfield, Painesville and on to Cleveland. The only thorough, broad, well appointed stage coach that passed over this route, was one McElvane. It was the fast mail train of those days, for two reasons—first, because it was *white*, and secondly, because of its speed, going the entire distance of one hundred and fifty miles in *one week*.

Mark the contrast between them, and now what a wonderful change. One can hardly realize it. Then the mail carrier, with the small bag upon his back, trudged on foot the entire distance; through swamps and dark and lonely forests, swimming the swollen streams and fording the shallow ones, creeping on logs for bridges and sleeping on boughs for beds—the carrier went his rounds and faithfully delivered the few letters and papers which were received and read by the early settlers. There were no "Dailies" then, and the "Weeklies" were read a month after they were printed.

Now the iron horse is hitched to the mail train, and with the velocity of the wind goes thundering across the continent, drawing tons of matter and leaving it at night hundreds of miles away from the starting point in the morning. The Dailies of our great cities are read before they are dry from the press.

The first permanent settlement in this township, was made in 1803, and the township was organized in 1811. I do not propose to enter upon a careful history of the settlement and early incidents of the township, that was most faithfully done twenty-five years ago to-day, by your then speaker, the Hon. J. R. Giddings, who had been one of the early settlers and could speak from actual knowledge and observation. Nor will I repeat that history. But changes have been wrought since the historian stood here at the close of the half century of the settlement of your township. Death has been busy in making those changes, and your community has borne a rich harvest for your cemeteries of fully ripened sheaves. The early settlers, have all, save one, been gathered to their fathers, and you are their children, grandchildren and great-grandchildren, are here to enjoy the fruits of their manly toil and cherish their memory. Do you realize what that toil was? They turned their backs upon homes where privileges abounded, homes of civilization and comfort, homes of religious, educational and political advantages, and came to these wilds, filled with beasts and Indians, to carve out for themselves new homes, and to undergo all of the hardships incident to the settlement of an untrodden land.

In doing this, they carved out for themselves a noble fame, and one that shall grow brighter as the years grow older.

The Pilgrim Fathers left a land which no longer furnished them a home, and came across the ocean from oppression that they might build for themselves altars of freedom.

Your fathers left homes of freedom, where they could be freemen; leaving lives of comparative ease, they sought in these western wilds, through lives of hardship and unrestrained toil, to lay broad and deep the foundations of a great state. There were no homes until they could make them, no schools until they could found them, no churches until they could rear them, and no fields until they could clear them. There were no means of communicating with the homes they had left, for there were then no post offices.

If the young men wished to correspond with loved ones left behind, they could not write them dainty letters on gilt-edged, rose-scented paper, and take them up to the post office for the morning's mail, in order that they might reach their destination by the next evening; they were forced to wait until some one of the community should be returning to the land of their fathers, when they would send such messages as the visiting person could conveniently carry.

The first post office established in the township was in 1825, in yonder house, with Hon. Miner as postmaster, and a distribution of letters and papers once a week. The first mails were carried by persons going on foot. Since then, even, most wonderous changes have been wrought. Then there were no fast freight trains to land the household effects from Connecticut at your doors in thirty-six hours. The fast freight train then consisted of a yoke of oxen hitched to a wagon, and your goods from New England were landed here after a journey lasting from three to six weeks. Then Steam Engines for drawing cars were unknown, so were reaping and mowing machines. No such machines as that represented in the picture hanging on that tree were then known, much less in use.

After sowing the grain they were forced to cut it with the old fashioned cradle, or by the less effective instrument the sickle, and the grass was cut with the hand-scythe and raked with the hand-rake. Not until 1833, when Hussey, of Ohio, invented the saw-tooth cutter, did you have machines for cutting grain and hay, and not until 1851, when W. H. Seymour, of New York, invented the reaping machine, did you have a machine that would gather the grain into form for binding, while now the most ingenious machine, of W. A. Wood, will cut, gather and bind into sheaves the grain.

Then there were no seed sowers, except such as Nature provided in the two hands of man; no grain drills to plant the seed in continuous rows; no sulkey hay-rakes upon which the driver sits while laboring, and upon which he can sit and take his noon nap.

Wayne was settled before Fulton had made the discovery of how to make steam effective.

It was not until 1808 that a steamboat became successful, when the "Clermont" successfully navigated the water.

In 1808 the "Phœnix" was taken by Stevens from New York,

by sea around to the Delaware River. It was the first voyage of a steamboat on the ocean. Not until 1819 was the ocean crossed by a Steam Craft, at which time the "Savannah" crossed from the city of Savannah to St. Petersburgh, and made the return trip to New York, taking twenty-six days for the return.

Now our floating palaces make the trip in eight or nine days time.

Then there was not a mile of railway on the continent; no Engine to screech in your ear, and no thundering train to disturb your slumbers. Over all that settled portion of our country, the horse was the means of the fastest locomotion. The first rail road in the country was built from Quincy, Mass., to tide water, in 1826, four miles long. Nor was it laid with the famous T rail. Its rail consisted of timbers three and a half inches wide, laid upon sleepers, and upon this timber was spiked a band of iron one-fourth of an inch thick. Nor was there a locomotive to hitch to the cars which rolled along this novel track, they were drawn by horses at the rate of four or five miles per hour.

The second rail road was built from Mauch Chunk to the Lehigh River, in 1827, a distance of thirteen miles. This was also a wooden railway and run by horses.

The first locomotive to draw cars by steam, was built in England, and landed in this country in 1830. It was a crude affair as compared with the things of almost marvelous beauty, and certainly of almost limitless power, which go tearing across our continent at the rate of thirty miles per hour, drawing trains which astonish one to behold.

When you met here twenty-five years ago, to celebrate the Semi-Centennial, there were 15,000 miles of railway in operation in this country, and in 1874 there were 72,623 miles, and now there are somewhere near 80,000 miles, costing between $4,000,000,000 and $5,000,000,000. The roads now in operation in the United States and Territories, if placed in one continuous line would extend around the globe more than three and one-quarter times.

A fourth of a century ago, it took from seventy to ninety days to cross our continent, and now the journey is accomplished in seven or eight days.

At that time, if any person had predicted that in a few years we should travel from Maine to California by steam, he would have been thought mad or insane; now the iron track stretches away from New England, across New York, the Middle and Western States, over the Mississippi, on to and over the great alkaline plains, through deep canyons and over mountain ranges, until it ends at the blue waters of the Pacific Ocean; and almost hourly the iron horse drags its load of freight or of human beings over mountain summits more than a mile and a half higher than the tallest church spire on the continent.

But the wonderful skill of man, stops not with laying the track *over* the mountain; it disdains to always climb, so it bores its way *through* the mountain and lays the track, and runs the engine through the opening.

But the inventive genius of man, stops not with the discovery of how to apply steam to the propelling of boats and the drawing of cars, for it has gone out into other fields and dealt with other agencies more subtle as well as more powerful. I said to you a few minutes ago, that the man who, twenty-five years ago, had prophesied that locomotives would draw long trains of cars over the Rocky and Sierra Nevada Mountains, would have been pronounced a fool or crazy. Yet we have seen the fulfillment of such predictions; but what would have been said of one, who, forty-five years ago, announced his belief that intelligence would be conveyed across the continent in a moment of time? So wild would the prediction been thought, that we would hardly have considered it worth while to spend time to laugh at the absurd notion.

Behold! the fulfillment of such wild notions, when in 1844 Prof. Morse sent over the wires from Baltimore to Washington, the words, "What hath God wrought?" The world was amazed and confounded. Yet, in the short space of thirty-four years, what astonishing results have been reached in the transmission of ideas over telegraph wires.

Now there are more than 214,000 miles of wire used for telegraph purposes in the United States, and on the globe there are more than 978,500 miles of wire, or enough to girdle the world more than thirty-nine times.

Long after your township was settled, if one of you received a letter announcing that some dear friend was dying at the old home, in New England, you would fully realize that in all human probability, long before you could reach the old homestead the dear one would be in the grave; but now, rapid as lightning, there flies across the states the words, "father is dying, come," and you take the afternoon train, and within twenty-four hours have reached almost any point in New England. The sad words may reach you away in Colorado, but you take the express train and reach the house of death in time for the funeral.

So rapid is intelligence now conveyed, that on receiving a dispatch from London, you look at the clock and compare the moment of sending with the exact time of its receipt, and are astonished to find by your time, it was received several hours earlier than it was sent.

The ingenuity of man stopped not with stretching the wire across rivers, gulfs and over mountain heights, it must press forward with resistless energy until continent should be bound to continent. Long years ago, it taught us how to spread forth the white canvass to the gale and make the trackless deep a highway o'er the world, but it was reserved for our day and generation to witness the astonishing, nay, almost miraculous feat of sending from the very sunrise of the eastern continent, under the ocean and to the very sunset of the western, an "All Hail," or a "God Speed," in a moment of time.

In 1858 the first ocean telegraph was laid, and the Queen of England and the President of the United States exchanged salutations, but in a short time it failed. In 1865 a second attempt was made to lay another, but it parted in mid ocean.

In 1866 another wire was successfully laid, and the ship from which it was paid out, returned to where the one of 1865 parted, and there the wonderful feat was performed of grappling the broken ends in water more than 6,000 feet deep, and bringing them to the surface and splicing them and completing the laying of the entire wire. There are miles enough of submarine cable now laid to encircle the globe more than two and one-fourth times.

These are days of mighty changes and events. The steamboat, locomotive and telegraph are now things of the past. The skill of man is making gigantic strides upon what has hitherto been unexplored fields. Already the world is standing in amazement at the telephone, phonograph and other achievements. I will venture no prediction, but if some Edison should appear here at the celebration of the completion of a full century of your township's history, and in some manner, bottle up the remarks of your then speakers, and lay them away to be reproduced, perfect in everything, a hundred years after, the world would be no more astonished than it has been at some of the brilliant successes of the past.

Wayne has never, so far as my knowledge goes, been very much given to aiding, in a business way, the class of professional men to which I belong.

The only lawyer who ever attempted to live in your midst, and carry on his profession, soon starved out, and moved to Jefferson.

It could not be said of Wayne what an old gentleman once said of the place where I reside. I will tell you the story.

One day, an old man, whom most of you knew for many years, went to Jefferson on business, connected with reducing his tax list. He was bent with age, stiffened with years of labor, and hobbled around with a cane in either hand. He was unsuccessful in his undertaking, and became irritated. He thought the lawyers were at the bottom of his difficulty. After leaving the Court House, he hobbled across the street to the East side, and then turning round called out to several legal gentlemen who were standing on the steps in front of the court house, in his squeaking voice, and said,. "I have known Jefferson when the wolves were very thick and the lawyers were very scarce, and now the lawyers are very thick and the wolves are very scarce, and the change has not benefited the place, either—hey!"

Since you met here twenty-five years ago, mighty events have transpired in the political world. The smoldering fires that were then burning have since broken out into fierce flames, and fanned by prejudice and passion, have burned with an intensity of heat that none of you then dreamed of. The tremendous conflict which was then raging between liberty and bondage, culminated in one of the bloodiest rebellions that ever drenched a land with blood. In that conflict were arrayed, upon one side those who desired to found a government upon human slavery, and upon the other those who desired freedom for all. I need not stop to say upon which side in that conflict you were arrayed. You fought for your convictions, and faithfully did you battle for truth, freedom and your country's integrity. Your sons and husbands and fathers carried the old flag upon more than six hundred battle fields and skirmish grounds, during that terrible conflict, and, true to the last, you bravely fought until you nobly won. But the long agony is over, and we may say with our own poet, Holmes,

> "Peace, with her large and lillied calms,
> "Like moonlight sits on land and lake,
> "With healing in her dewy balms
> "For pride that pines and hearts that ache,
> "From Huron to the land of palms."
>
> "From rock-bound Massachusetts bay
> "To San Francisco's golden gate;
> "From where Itasca's waters play,
> "To those that plunge and palpitate
> "A thousand happy leagues away,
> "And drink amid her dunes and bars
> "The Mississippi's boiling tide,
> "Still floating from a million spars
> "The Nation's Ensign undefied
> "Blazons her galaxy of stars."

Time rolls on! Most of the old settlers are gone; but they left their impress upon everything connected with your township. In you I see worthy sons and daughters of worthy sires. A few of those who helped to clear your fields and rear your homes are still with you. They are the links in the chain which binds you to the past. Care for them, gently lead them during their short stay, that their last days may be peaceful.

Of those who took part in your ceremonies twenty-five years ago, many are gone, a few are left. Your then speaker has gone from scenes of bitterest strife to his great reward. It fell to his lot in this life to be a prominent figure during the most exciting period of our country's history. When he addressed you here, the principles for which he was contending in the councils of the nation were most unpopular. He was almost alone in advocating them then. Social ostracism was visited upon him and yet he faltered not. He saw not the end, but hoped when all seemed dark. In the moral and political world, as in the physical, there is a seed time and a harvest, and we may know as surely in one as in the other, that what we sow we shall also gather; but we may not know in one as we know in the other when that harvest shall be. In the physical world we go forth at spring time and scatter the seed with the full knowledge that in the summer or autumn we shall reap the golden grain; in the moral or political world we go forth to the seed time, but God alone knows when the harvest shall be. That it shall surely come is decreed of heaven. That which is planted may lay for years unseen by mortal eyes, unheard by mortal ears, but watched and watered by care eternal it shall bloom in other years, and in the far off harvest fields shall be gathered the golden grain.

Mr. Giddings had then gone forth to the seed time and was planting the slowly sprouting seed of human rights, but he could not tell what generation should go forth to the reaping. That which he planted bloomed again before he was gathered to his fathers. But it bloomed amid the red fields of blood, and above three hundred thousand swarded war mounds.

"'Tis thus Omnipotence its law fulfills,
"And vengence executes what Justice wills."

But the brave man has gone; yet he lives in all that exalts a people or makes a nation grand—even unto immortal fame—while millions of free hearts beat off a grand anthem to his praise.

Another one of your speakers then (Rev. E. B. Chamberlain) has lived to address you to-day. His words have been words of wisdom, and it will be well that you give heed to them. You have loved him during the years that are passed, and I know your love goes out to him to-day. He has been with many of you at your marriage, with many of your dear friends at death, and has shared with you many of the joys and sorrows of life. I know your earnest prayer is that his life may yet be spared to him these many years, and that he may be crowned with blessings while he lives and with that better life after death.

One other prominent figure in your gathering twenty-five years ago, is here to-day. I allude to the one who was your Chairman and President of the day, Mr. C. C. Wick. He comes back to you now to find so much that has changed. Many of his *old* companions are gone, and his young ones have grown old. In yonder cemetery are resting some who were as dear to him as his own life, and many who were very near to him as neighbors and friends; and there too he hopes to rest when he shall receive the not unwelcome summons to "come home." May he be blest with lengthened years which shall be full of happiness.

When your President called for all who were here then, to arise, I looked on with mingled feelings of pleasure and sadness. Pleasure, that so many have been spared, and sadness, when I thought how few of all that number, will live to join in your full Centennial. What may await us all I know not; what of happiness or sorrow may be in store for you is not given unto me to tell, but permit me, in closing, to express the hope, that as your lives have been peaceful and prosperous, so may they continue to be full of blessings, that at the close, you may look back over years that have been overflowing with the richness of life, and be able to say, I have fought the good fight.

The close of Mr. Northway's speech brought forth from those who had listened attentively, prolonged cheers, making the " wild woods ring," which only ceased when a song by the ancient choir was announced, and

"Why do we mourn departing friends"

was sung to the tune *China.*

Judge Cadwell, of Cleveland, being present, was introduced, and told us some incidents of the early settlements, also several anecdotes in his usual happy manner.

The Wayne Choir then sang

"Hark the song of Jubilee,"

after which the historian, Uncle Linus H. Jones, came forward and read a sketch of the history of the township for the twenty five years past.

ADDRESS

—OF—

LINUS H. JONES.

Mr. President, Fellow Citizens and Friends:—It is with no little emotion that I arise to address you in a duty which the occasion appears to demand. Knowing full well that you will not look for anything from me to be garnished with eloquence, in language or manner, I venture upon somewhat of a review of our history as a township for the past twenty-five years—we were then told, that

> "Half centuries were the small dots
> On time's broad dial-plate;
> Way-marks set up to show the world
> How early or how late."

Although this is true in regard to the general course of time, yet, in regard to man, it measures more than half of a full life time. Wherefore, when we take survey of a period embracing but three-fourths of a century, a twenty-five, or a ten to five become prominent marks or dots by which we compute or measure its course.

In looking over the record of twenty-five years ago, which takes up our history from the time that the woodman's ax first resounded in the forests of Wayne, relating the slow and toilsome progress of clearing the land of its heavy timber, which then covered every acre of our township, before anything could be done in producing by cultivation, the advent of families here and there making openings in the dense forests, and happy when they had succeeded in driving the forest back to such a distance that the tall trees could not, in falling, reach the log cabin, nor obstruct the direct rays of the sun. A patch of corn planted by striking an ax into the ground, dropping the seed into the opening, and then closed by a pressure of the foot. Recounting various privations and hardships, and the advance of improvements in bringing the land into a condition to be serviceable for the sustenance of man and beast—the general progress, agriculturally, socially, civilly and religiously, for fifty years, which may be considered more than the full time of our minority, which brought us to the period when we held a place as a settled township, and fully established in the routine and humdrum of agricultural life, all moving (with few exceptions) in the same grove, having a common interest with each other in the improvements of the times, which were largely the making of roads, providing for schools, Gospel privileges, etc., at a time when incessant and laborious toil was necessary in order to obtain the ordinary means of sustenance. This having been told, it appears to cover that part of our history which is distinctly the period of improvement and change, more than is usual in a course of years which would follow.

We cannot detail to you the change from forest to field, the change from the log cabin to comely farm house, or the log schoolhouse, with windows of oiled paper, to those of a more comely aspect; *that* belongs to our previous history. Here I may state that the building of good houses commenced something over fifty years ago. The house now occupied by F. E. Jones, was built in 1826, by Samuel Jones, Sr., and was probably the best at the time. The one now occupied by the Kennedys, was built near that time, by Anson Jones, a brother of the lamented Drayton Jones; afterwards occupied successively by Sela Whiting, Gordon Miller and the parents of the present occupants. Thus the change went on, when at the close of our fiftieth year, the log buildings had nearly all disappeared.

Within the past twenty-five years many good houses have been built, prominent among which are those of Chester Oatman, E. A. Fobes, O. P. Fobes and many others that belong to the class of good farm houses. A large number of the early built and less pretentious houses have been enlarged and improved in a manner which shows enterprise and thrift, giving our township the appearance of a generally well-to-do community, without being able to boast of the millionaire or $100,000 man, with his stately mansion. Two dwellings have been consumed by fire, one belonging to Rufus Woodworth, eight or ten years ago, and the Hezekiah Platt house, owned and occupied by Charles Smith. In churches, the loss of the Congregational Church, by fire, December, 1872, incurring a loss of about $4,000. Our present house, built in 1874, at an expense of over $6,400, stands in its place. The Methodist Church was 'moved from Lindenville to the Center in 1865, enlarged, reseated and improved to its present comely aspect. Those who knew Wayne from passing through it twenty-five years ago, would know it now, but would not say, it is going down.

We pause here and look around for the veterans of twenty-five years ago; where are they?

Capt. Joshua Fobes and wife, Deacon Calvin Andrews, Elisha Giddings and wife, Hori Miner and wife, widow Titus Hayes, Mrs. Samuel Jones, Deacon Wm. Fitch and wife, Deacon Simon Fobes, Levi Fobes and wife, Deacon Norman Wilcox and wife, Rev. Ephraim T. Woodruff and wife, Dr. Luther Spellman and wife, Jerry Hart and wife, Nathaniel Coleman and wife, Charles Walworth and wife, and David Fobes, all of the above named were near the age of seventy years, some more and some less, at the time of our Semi-Centennial.

Those who took a prominent place upon the platform were Hon. J. R. Giddings, Rev. H. A. Babcock, Rev. George Roberts. I can extend the list. We may look and think. We find one left of that group who had numbered three score and ten years, has outlived his generation and stands tottering upon the grave's brink. We think them over as we knew them twenty-five years ago; our hearts sadden as we run over the extended list, and yet nothing more has taken place than was looked for in the natural course of events. But our task in this vein is but begun; we may note of those then with us, Albigence Woodworth and wife, Horatio Woodworth, Charles Spellman, Cyrus Camp and wife, Wm. Matthews, H. G. Dean and wife, David Smilie and wife, Loton Fobes, Oshea Fobes and wife, Sylvester Ward and wife, Mrs. C. C. Wick, Augustus Ward, Hezekiah Platt and wife, Leroy Hayes, Dr. Bradley and wife, Mrs. Charlotte Hayes, (Weeks,) Mrs. Philemon Brockway, all of whom left families at about or quite mature age, and at this time, if living, would each have numbered, at the least, three score years to that of about eighty-five to ninety. As we cast a look back, memory brings up the recollection of James W. Kennedy, Billings Barber, Mrs. Anson Jones, Mrs. Samuel Jones, Jr., Milton R. Miner, Eli Barton and wife, Mrs. Rufus Woodworth, Mrs. Amasa Woodworth, George Marvin, Henry P. Wilder, Mrs. Joel Pease, Mrs. H. A. Babcock, mostly of a younger class, who then stood with us, with prospects as fair for this day as many of us at that time, who are permitted to enjoy this occasion.

The review of the past calls up mingled emotions of pleasure and sadness; of *pleasure* that so large a number of the residents of former days can greet each other on so memorable an occasion; of *sadness*, when we think of the vacancies which time has made in our ranks of twenty-five years ago.

Thus has the unyielding, but steady pressure of the hand of time been forcing us along, until those who bore the hardships of pioneer life and their peers in years have been forced out of life, while those who then stood firm in manhood's prime have become the old of to-day. No sweeping sickness has thinned our ranks. True, in January, 1877, the small pox made its appearance, causing our whole population to stand aghast; but, by prudence and care, a fearful effect was avoided, except in two families, those of Franklin Niles and Lyman H. Fobes, from one of which three were removed by death, and of severe cases we note those of Wm. S. McGranahan and F. A. Kinnear. We may look over the times of our late war, and call to mind the anxieties and forebodings which stirred our hearts to their very depths, when our sons and brothers were called to the field of conflict, the anguish of spirit when the tidings came that one and another had fallen, yet we have occasion for gratitude and thanksgiving, to-day, that our bereavement was so much less than many of our sister townships. The loss, by death, of those accredited to this township was made to be fifteen, among whom were Frederick M. Giddings, Ferdinand F. Fobes, Albert G. Rowe, Wm. Bradenbaugh, Newton Woodworth, Charles Smith, Claudius Steele, Nathaniel Latham Coleman, L. A. Monta, John Roberts, Geo. W. Northrup, Orlando O. Wakeman, and David B. Montgomery. We look over this past record with feelings of sadness, bringing together in one view the admonitions of our mortality; yet we have occasion to be grateful for so great a preservation of life, and so bounteous a supply of all that is necessary to contribute to human happiness and comfort, closing our seventy-fifth year with an abundance of the products of the field to that extent that future want must be far in the distance.

We pause here and look around for those who remain of the early settlers that were with us twenty-five years ago. On the east, we find Diodate Woodworth, aged eighty-seven years. Of those who lived on the Hayes road, we find Samuel Jones, aged ninety-seven years, Mrs. Calvin Andrews, lately gone to Kansas, Mrs. Jabez Fobes, Mrs. Sally Barber, and west we find Amasa Woodworth, Mrs. Dolly Fobes, and Mrs. Rosanna Lowery, aged ninety years. [Of those then with us, who were less than sixty years of age, and now over sixty-five, (with few exceptions,) we notice the following; Horace Wilcox and wife, (Mary Fobes, the first female child born in the township,) Deacon L. E. Parker, (died Jan. 2nd, 1879,) and wife, Deacon David Parker and wife, Richard Hayes and wife, Horace F. Giddings and wife, Linus H. Jones and wife, Philip Fonner and wife, Dr. C. B. Walworth and wife, Anson Jones, Mrs. Elizabeth Thompson, (formerly Mrs. Matthews,) Nathaniel Coleman and wife, Jerry Wilcox and wife, Norman Wilcox and wife, David Hart and wife, Joel Pease, Mrs. Rosetta McMichael, Mrs. Henry Wilder, George Wakeman and wife, Simon P. Fobes and wife, and just over the border, Anson J. Giddings and wife, and Joshua H. Giddings and wife.]

About seventeen years ago, note was made that eighteen persons were living in the township, within one mile of the Pymatuning, whose average ages were over eighty years.

Comparatively few of the homesteads have passed from the possession of the descendants of their early occupants, except some of short continuance. Some of the exceptions are that of Rufus Woodworth, in lots twenty-nine and thirty, E. T. Woodruff, Deacon Calvin Andrews, Hezekiah Platt, Benoni Andrews, Samuel Jones, Jr., (now owned by D. T. Beardsley,) and some others of less note. In the western half, most of the homesteads are occupied by those who first settled or occupied them, that part having been settled at a much later period.

Among the changes which have taken place, we may notice some of the inroads of that tyrant, fashion. We need not go back and notice the change from four and a half yards for a lady's dress, to that of eight or ten, and our appreciation of the improvement in graceful style becoming a lady; but when the expansive period arrived, with its baloon proportions, and the consequent increase of fabric to sixteen and twenty or more yards, in order to cover the ribby frame, we were put to our wits' end as to what was about to happen. One suggestion was that the ladies had become Millerites and were preparing for the ascension. But it proved that Miller had miscalculated, the bubble burst with a consequent collapse, which the sterner sex looked upon with favor, as having the effect of diminishing the bill for material. But here we were doomed to disappointment, for now the wits were set to work to devise plans to use up the material, a wudge is made here, a fold or two there, with some six or eight pull-ups, and a wrap or two, until we imagine the dressmaker to say, "There, that won't look bad," and the anxiety of the *how* is relieved. But however much we may be disposed to criticise, we must accord to the ladies one exhibition of sense and good taste, in rejecting the bloomer innovation, about thirty years ago. We could not resist the impression, when seeing one thus attired, that she exhibited herself as influenced by masculine aspirations.

We might go back and speak of what were called bonnets, their ample dimensions enveloping the lady's head and face so perfectly that one could not catch a glimpse of the twinkling eye, or pouting lips, without some favoritism, except by a square look, and the palm of the hand was sufficent to hide the modest blushes, somewhat to our annoyance in younger days. We will not detail the main changes; we recollect the sky rakers that came within our period, which induced an upward look, the gradual diminution of size to that of *hat*, its gradual rise to the top of the head, till now it sits above it, as a top-not, giving a full view of the radiant face, which seems to invite an approach from any angle you may desire.

We will not farther contrast the past with the present. We have arrived at our present condition by slow and toilsome progress, and without the fluctuations which have been common in late years, and are fully settled down as a rural township, without a railroad, but plenty of them at our very door, and no great change is to be looked for, more than is common in such a position, unless some enterprising adventurer should "strike ile."

Although we are through with our review, we cannot forbear casting a glance forward, and ask ourselves, what will Wayne be when she has completed her century? We look upon those now in active life; those who may remain will be the old of that day; those now in their teens, with those who have but lately attained to their major state, will then be the active men, each one contributing to the character and position which the township will have in our county and region. Therefore, I may say to those now in active life, and the younger who form the rear guard with the ranks of recruits, "come to the front," and make your township what you wish it to be, that you may indulge a just pride in saying and having it known, that your home is Wayne.

The Ancient Choir favored us with one more song—*Auld Lang Syne*—when all joined in singing *Old Hundred*.

On motion of Mr. Wm. B. Smilie the meeting adjourned for twenty-five years, after which the benediction was pronounced by Rev. E B. Chamberlain.

The following was written for the Anniversary, but was not presented in time to be read on that day, we therefore give it a place.—PUB. COMMITTEE.

THE GREETING.

We come, we come, from east and west,
And north and south we come;
We come to greet each long loved friend,
And loved old home.

Dear, loved old *Wayne!* thy pleasant lands
And hills of gentle height,
Crowned with abodes of peace and love,
Were a delight.

Cherished in memory's faithful page,
As back each leaf we turn,
Written as with a sunbeam there,
We quick discern

The same kind look, the welcome kind
    That met us oft before,
The same kind pressure of the hand
    We feel once more.

Ah, there are those we'll ne'er forget—
    Whose friendship tried and true,
Has left a solace in our hearts—
    They've passed from view.

Not lost to us, Oh no! not lost,
    But only gone before;
They wait to welcome coming ones
    On the other shore.

Oh! when our meeting days are o'er,
    And parting comes at last,
Be ours the joy to meet again,
    When time has passed.

Then in the kingdom of our Lord,
    With joy each other greet,
Joining in praise with one accord,
    Bowing at his feet.

THE RESPONSE.

Welcome, dear friends; we join in friendly greeting ;
Welcome, thrice welcome to our happy meeting.
'Tis cause of joy that we may celebrate
This Anniversary of our early date.
Seventy-five years have passed since came
Our parents settling in the town of Wayne,
And we with gratitude would now record
The never-ceasing goodness of our Lord.
Let sweet thanksgiving rise in grateful song,
Adoring praise from every heart and tongue ;
Thus will our friendship be renewed,
Though miles divide us nothing need intrude
To break the chain which ever bright may be
Reaching from time into eternity.

Those dear ones! whom Heaven has called away
To rest, in waiting for the coming day,
With love and reverence we their memory keep,
Trusting the Lord to break the last long sleep,
And bring us each, with those who've gone before,
Into His kingdom, to go out no more.

                By MRS. L. C. BEARSS.

CASUALTIES.

June, 1840.—As Mrs. Dr. Allen, of Kinsman, was driving east on the road from the gothic school house, her horse became frightened and unmanageable, and she was thrown with such force against the fence as to break both her limbs and one arm. She was taken to the house of Justus Fobes where she died in about six hours.

Nov., 1848.—Drayton Jones fell through the scaffold over the barn floor, alighting on the cylinder of a thrashing machine while it was in motion. He was torn and mangled in a shocking manner; he lived, however, about four days.

Sept. 29th, 1850.—Henry Wilder, a young man from Sorrel Hill, Pa., who was working for Daniel Haines, on lot No. ninety-one, was killed by lightning. It was in the evening, and the entire family was in the room, and he was in the act of drawing a plan of his father's house on the stove, when the fluid passed down the pipe, tearing the stove into fragments and scattering the pieces around the room. The rest of the family was more or less injured.

Feb. 14th, 1854.—Lodema Andrews, daughter of Samuel Andrews, was scalded to death. Aged 20 years.

July 4th, 1857.—Lysander W. Fobes was killed by the premature discharge of a cannon, while firing a salute at sunrise. Aged 27 years.

Nov., 1864.—J. T. Miner, was assisting in raising a bent for an addition to a barn belonging to Wm. Kiddle, on lot No. eighty-eight, when by some mismanagement the bent fell to the ground, crushing him badly. He lived about one week.

SUICIDES.

1823.—Stephen Inman hung himself by resting his neck on a piece of elm bark stretched from a stump to a stake, on lot No. eighty-six.

Feb. 7th, 1853.—Mr. John Kennedy came to his death by the shot of a gun, supposed to have been discharged by his own hands. Aged 56 years.

Sept., 1857.—Frank Lyman, of Cherry Valley, poisoned himself by drinking morphine mixed with water, at the residence of Eliphlet Clark, on lot No. eighty-eight.

1849.—Charles Grokenbarger hung himself in an ashery building, near the town line between Wayne and Cherry Valley.

1821.—The grist mill in the south-east part of the township, on the Pymatuning Creek, was completed. It was an improvement much needed at that time.

Sept. 13th, 1878.—There occurred the greatest flood ever known here. The Pymatuning Creek was higher by twelve or fifteen inches than ever known before, sweeping its flats entirely clean of fences and bridges, causing much damage to roads, &c

Summer of 1808.—A severe wind storm passed over this town. Its track was about a half mile wide, and extended from about a mile north of the center in a direction a little south of east, and terminated just before reaching the Pymatuning. It completely prostrated the timber in its course.

DEATHS.

The following is the miscellaneous list of the deaths among the *old* Settlers and their descendants, from the first settlement of the township, and in some instances it has been followed down to the present time, yet the list does not embrace all, especially those who came to the township at a more recent date; but it is more extended than was at first anticipated, and will be found as nearly correct as could well be made from the information obtained from the friends of the deceased and from other sources.

Simon Fobes 1st, died Feb. 7th, 1808, aged 86 years; Thankful, his wife, died Feb. 4th, 1808, aged 87 years; Bethiah, daughter of Simon 1st and Thankful Fobes, died Sept. 15th, 1836, aged 82 years.

Simon Fobes 2nd, died Jan. 30th, 1840, aged 84 years; Elizabeth, his wife, died July 18th, 1837, aged 79 years. Simon Fobes 3rd, died Feb. 8th, 1861, aged 77 years; Sylvia H., his wife, died Dec. 14th, 1842, aged 51 years; Deidamia, second wife, died April 10th, 1856; and of the children of Simon 3rd and Sylvia H. Fobes, Dr. Abial J. Fobes, died April 1st, 1851, aged 32 years; Louisa, his wife, died April 8th, 1851, aged 33 years; Lois L., wife of Dwight Coe, died Jan. 1st, 1869, aged 39 years; Lucy A., wife of F. B. Fitch, died at Brighton, Cal., Dec. 1st, 1877, aged 52 years; and of the children of Simon Fobes 4th and Catherine A., Ferdinand Fobes died at Murfreesborough Sept. 4th, 1863, aged 21 years; Maggie, wife of L. L. Fobes, died Sept. 7th, 1877, aged 35 years; and of the children of Orlando P. and Nancy Fobes, Hettie L. died Feb. 20th, 1867, aged 3 years; also Birtie B. died March 16th, 1872, aged 6 years, making the sixth generation of this branch of the Fobes family that are buried in the cemetery at the center of the town.

Levi Fobes died Nov. 5th, 1869, aged 81 years; Eunice, his wife, died April 4th, 1871, aged 78 years; and of the children of Levi and Eunice Fobes, Levi J. Fobes died Nov. 28th, 1856, aged 41 years; Vastia, his wife, died Sept. 22nd, 1872, aged 54 years; Elizabeth, wife of O. H. Miner, died May 24th, 1843, aged 23 years, also two infant children died at the same time; Celia, also wife of O. H. Miner, died Feb. 21st, 1862, aged 38 years; Amelia, wife of Lyman Bentley, died Nov. 8th, 1858, aged 44 years; Orrin Fobes died July 24th, 1861, aged 38 years; Lysander W. Fobes died July 4th, 1857, aged 27 years.

Joshua Fobes died Sept. 16th, 1861, aged 80 years; Dorothy, his wife, died Jan. 25th, 1873, aged 93 years; and of the children of Joshua and Dorothy Fobes, Alvin Fobes died May 1st, 1840, aged 36 years; Emily, wife of Joshua, Jr., died Feb. 3rd, 1847, aged 35 years.

THE FAMILY OF NATHAN FOBES, OF CHESTER, MASS.

Nathan Fobes died 1833, aged 76 years, Rebecca, his wife, died

1827, aged 72 years; David Fobes died 1865, aged 82 years; Anna, his wife, died 1839; Electa Fobes *Foster* died April 30th, 1853, aged 34 years; Sophia Fobes *Farver*—no dates; Jabez Fobes died April 16th, 1857, aged 73 years; Sarah Fobes *Mapes* still living, aged 87 years; Joseph Fobes died Oct. 12th, 1850, aged 31 years; Julia Fobes *Phillips*—no dates; Nathan Fobes 2nd died Feb , 1813; Justus Fobes died 1868, aged 80 years; Philotheta, his wife, died—no dates; Amoret Fobes died 1863; Elisha Fobes—no dates; Loton Fobes died Jan. 3rd, 1863, aged 67 years; Dolly, his wife, still living, aged 81 years; Aurora Fobes died May 24th, 1846, aged 20 years; Oshea Fobes died March 10th. 1869, aged 72 years; Abigal, his wife, died Feb. 13th. 1871, aged 72 years; William P. Fobes died Dec. 3rd, 1873, aged 51 years.

Elisha Giddings, wife, Philotheta, and son, Anson J., came to this town in 1805, where ten more children were born, all of whom reached manhood and womanhood, and were married before ary deaths occurred among their number. They have a numerous progeny. Ashtabula county being the home of many branches of the family. Elisha Giddings died August 9th, 1855, aged 75 years; His wife, Philotheta, died Dec. 24th, 1868, aged 86 years; of their children, Sidney died Oct. 18th, 1851, aged 36 years; Polly, wife of Sidney, died July 12th, 1862, aged 38 years; Sophia *Mosely* died March 15th, 1847, aged 26 years; Philotheta *Hayes* died Oct. 2nd, 1851, aged 27 years; Seth H. died July 16th, 1849, aged 23 years; of their grand children, all of Anson J.'s children are dead, namely: Addison L. died Sept. 30th, 1851, aged 12 years; A. Eugene died July 30th, 1866, aged 23 years, from disease contracted while in the Union Army. Lucian A. died Jan. 12th, 1867, aged 21 years; Sarah A. died April 26th, 1868, aged 20 years.

Frederick M., son of Horace F., died at Murfreesborough, Tenn., April 21st, 1863, aged 28 years.

Charles, son of J. Marvin, died in the Army, Nov. 24th, 1862, aged 20 years.

Joshua Giddings and family came to this town in 1806. He died about the year 1833, aged about 75; his wife, Elizabeth, died about 1830, aged near 70; of their children, Aranda P., died about 1843; Hon. Joshua R. Giddings died at Montreal, Canada, May

27th, 1864, where he held the position of United States Consul to Canada, having received his appointment at the hands of President Lincoln, in 1861.

J. Warren Giddings died April 20th, 1861, aged 72 years; Esther, wife of Warren Giddings, died Oct. 29th, 1868, aged 78 years; Sarah *Boardwell*, daughter of Warren and Esther, died in the fall of 1875, aged 53 years; Willis Boardwell died Dec. 25th, 1876, aged about 53 years.

Daniel Palmer and family came to this town in 1835. He died May 26th, 1870, aged about 58 years; Marian, his wife, died July 15th, 1852.

Philemon Brockway died 1836, aged 57 years; Sally, his wife, died 1865, aged 79 years; Samuel Brockway died Oct., 1854; Ruby Brockway *Eastman* died 1862; Lucretia Brockway *Bacon* died 1874; Luman Brockway died Sept. 9th, 1863, aged 41 years.

Hon. Titus Hayes died Feb. 8th, 1832, aged 56 years; Phebe, his wife, died May 5th, 1865, aged 83 years; and of the children of Titus and Phebe Hayes, Leroy Hayes died Sept. 28th, 1863, aged 62 years; Charlotte, wife of Jeremiah Weeks, died Aug. 24th, 1871, aged 67 years; Jeremiah Weeks died Aug. 20th, 1864, aged 68 years; Phebe, wife of Wm. Leach, died March 7th, 1847, aged 25 years.

George Wakeman 1st died 1812, aged 56 years; Sarah, his wife, died 1842, aged 84 years; Samuel, son of George and Sarah, died 1852, aged 80 years; Ruth, his wife, died 1865, aged 82 years; George, son of Samuel and Ruth, and Welthey, his wife, still live, and reside on the lands settled by his father and grandfather. To them were born eight children; the fourth one, Orlando O., enlisted in Co. C, 29th Reg. O. V. I., Sept., 1861, died in Winchester Hospital April, 1862, aged 22 years.

Samuel Jones, Sr., now living, aged 98 years, settled in this town in 1811; Deborah, his wife, died Sept. 1st, 1863, aged 81 years; and of the children of Samuel and Deborah Jones, Flavel Jones died June 9th, 1842, aged 36 years; Orrilla (*Burton*), his wife, died Jan., 1868.

Lovel E. Parker died Jan. 2nd, 1879, aged 79 years; Statira, his wife, died May 23rd, 1839, aged 32 years.

Mary P., wife of Linus H. Jones, died Sept. 15th, 1828, aged 20 years; Eliza, second wife, died Jan. 15th, 1840, aged 37 years. Fannie B., wife of Anson Jones, died Jan. 4th, 1865, aged 54 years.

Dr. Thos. E. Best, (married Emily Jones,) died Oct. 5th, 1877, aged 67 years.

Samantha, wife of Samuel Jones, Jr., died Jan. 9th, 1866, aged 41 years.

Sylvia, wife of Flavel E. Jones, died March 13th, 1865, aged 25 years.

Sarah, wife of L. Newton Parker, died Dec. 17th, 1873, aged 32 years.

Deacon Nathaniel Coleman died May 17th, 1837, aged 83 years.

Nathaniel Coleman settled in Wayne in 1806, and died July 22nd, 1868, aged 90 years; Submit, his wife, died Jan: 1st, 1809, aged 27 years; Keziah, second wife, died Feb. 9th, 1862, aged 78 years;

Rachel Hoisington, daughter of Nathaniel and Keziah Coleman, died Sept. 12th, 1878, aged 64 years.

Keziah, wife of David Jones, died April 5th, 1823, aged 62 years.

William Jones died Dec. 11th, 1855, aged 68 years.

Eliphalet Phelps died March 10th, 1842, aged 76 years; Mahetabel, his wife, died Jan. 22nd, 1840, aged 74 years; Miss Harriet Phelps died 1852, aged 54 years.

The first settler on the Creek Road, (so called,) in Wayne, was Albigence Woodworth, in 1811, who died May 30th, 1874, aged 86 years; Sally, his wife, died in 1826, aged 34 years; Elizabeth *Allen*, second wife, died 1871, aged 65 years.

Ezra Woodworth died June 3rd, 1874, aged 66 years.

Diodate Woodworth settled in Wayne in 1812, and is still living on the place where first settled, aged 87 years; Julana, his wife, died March 4th, 1868, aged 67 years.

Horatio Woodworth died in 1863, aged 67 years; Charity, his wife, died in 1849, aged 49 years.

Newton Woodworth died in the army.

Charity Ketchum died———, aged 84 years.

Esther Ketchum died 1878, aged 84 years.

Rufus Woodworth still living; Jane, his wife, died in 1878; and of their children, Alexander Woodworth died Feb. 9th, 1858, aged 29 years; Roswell Woodworth died in 1858. John Woodworth died Jan. 1st, 1829; Sally, his wife, died 1839. Amasa Woodworth still living, aged 82 years; Lucy, his wife, died Aug. 22nd, 1870, aged 78 years. Dr. Luther Woodworth died Feb. 28th, 1853; Maria, his wife, died Nov., 1865, aged 49 years. Silas Babcock died Aug. 10th, 1843, aged 73 years—a soldier of 1812; Rachel, his wife, died Sept. 28th, 1834, aged 56 years; and their children, Dauphne *French* died Aug. 11th, 1816, aged 18 years; Hiram A. died June 1st, 1868, aged 66 years; Anna *Davidson* died July 6th, 1858, aged 58 years; Evelina *Babcock* died Aug. 23rd, 1853, aged 48 years; Orville died———, aged about 50 years; Rachel A. died Sept. 29th, 1875, aged 66 years; Daniel H. died Jan. 14th, 1873, aged 62 years; Sarah *Gibson* died———, aged about 50 years.

Wife and children of Hiram A.:—Eliza P. died July 22nd, 1871, aged 56 years; infant son died July 26th, aged 4 days; Anna Eliza died June 22nd, 1851, aged 4 years; Lyman Beecher died Dec. 25th, 1862, aged 19 years.

Wife and child of Silas A., son of Hiram A.:—Martha J., wife of Silas A., died Jan. 17th, 1873, aged 23 years. She was in usual health, and took a dose of chloral at the hand of Dr. B. H. Phelps to have a tooth pulled and died in the operation. Martha L. died Dec. 17th, 1874, aged 2 years.

Jerry Hart died Oct. 20th, 1857, aged 73 years; Lola, his wife, died Sept. 20th, 1866, aged 81 years; and of the children of Jerry and Lola Hart, Josiah Hart died Jan. 21st, 1848, aged 28 years; Jerry Hart died Dec. 29th, 1843, aged 28 years; Fidelia, wife of John Spellman, died June 22nd, 1842, aged 28 years; Phebe, wife of Leonard Tuttle, died Sept. 9th, 1854, aged 35 years; Submit, wife of David Hart, died May 6th, 1839, aged 28 years; Lola Hart died Dec. 19th, 1841, aged 18 years.

Dr. Luther Spellman died Sept. 3rd, 1863, aged 84 years; Anna, his wife, died March 12th, 1870, aged 86 years; and of the children of Dr. Luther and Anna Spellman, John Spellman died Dec. 17th,

1841, aged 23 years; Henry Spellman died Feb. 27th, 1867, aged 49 years; Truman Spellman died Jan. 6th, 1870, aged 22 years; Charles Spellman died Jan. 8th, 1875, aged 64 years; Luvia, his wife, died Aug. 6th, 1840, aged 29 years; Franklin Spellman died April 8th, 1852, aged 27 years; Sally, his wife, died April 1st, 1854, aged 29 years; Corintha *Palmer* died Feb. 20th, 1846, aged 39 years; Jane Woodworth died March 28th, 1859, aged 31 years.

Cyrus T. Camp died Dec. 11th, 1856, aged 81 years; Amoret, his wife, died 1837, aged 28 years; Delilah, second wife, died Dec. 15th, 1865, aged 56 years,

Benjamin Ward died April 14th, 1850, aged 86 years; Betsey, his wife, died May 4th, 1849, aged 74 years; and of the children of Benjamin and Betsey Ward, Sylvester Ward died Aug. 21st, 1866, aged 69 years; Eliza, his wife, died Feb. 22nd, 1872, aged 64 years.

Augustus Ward died Aug. 7th, 1851, aged 45 years.

Benjamin J. Ward died Nov. 22nd, 1874. aged 74 years; Samantha, his wife, died Feb. 18th, 1873, aged 56 years.

Matilda, wife of C. C. Wick, died July 7th, 1854, aged 42 years.

Orcutt R. Ward, son of Sylvester and Eliza Ward, died Jan. 2nd, 1879, aged 51 years.

Emily, wife of David Simpkins, died July 19th, 1861, aged 27 years.

Luman Bartholomew died June, 1832, aged 49 years; his wife, Ruth Ann, afterward Mrs. Roger Cadwell, died March, 1869, aged 85 years; Jasper H. died———1843, aged 36 years; Noah died June, 1862, aged 52 years; Clarissa *Ward*, first wife of Noah, died ———1841; Mariah *Ward*, second wife of Noah, died Jan., 1861, aged 52 years; Joseph L. died Feb., 1833, aged 19 years; Betsy *Cutler* died Aug., 1849, aged 33 years; Armina L. died———1831, aged 2 years; Luman, son of Betsy, died a prisoner at Bell Isle. Of the eighty-five descendants of Luman Bartholomew but one is now living who bears the family name, viz: Jason C., his oldest son, who now lives in Iowa. All have left this place.

Hori Miner was appointed the first Postmaster of Wayne, in Sept., 1825, and the same *month* settled on lot forty-eight, one-fourth mile north of Lindenville, on the Hayes road, where he held the office for twenty years, and there lived until the time of his death, Oct. 20th, 1874, aged 87 years; Permelia, his wife, died March 26th, 1871, aged 78 years; Milton R. Miner, son of Hori and Permelia Miner, died Jan. 6th, 1877, aged 55 years; Mary Jane, his wife, died July 20th, 1856, aged 27 years; Joseph Miner, also a son of Hori and Permelia Miner, died Sept, 6th, 1839, aged 7 years; William Miner, son of M. R. and M. J. Miner, died Nov. 13th, 1872, aged 27 years.

Christopher Miner died May 19th, 1865, aged 92 years; Matilda, his wife, died Jan. 28th, 1855, aged 82 years.

J. T. Miner died Nov., 1864, aged 57 years; Sarah, his wife, died May 16th, 1862, aged 45 years.

Deacon William Fitch died March 24th, 1876, aged 93 years; Amanda, his wife, died Jan. 15th, 1869, aged 85 years; and of the children of Wm. and Amanda Fitch, John S. Fitch died Dec. 16th, 1857, aged 35 years; Hez Lee Fitch died Oct. 9th, 1844, aged 27 years; Edward H. Fitch died Aug. 12th, 1839, aged 9 years.

Hezekiah Platt died Dec. 2nd, 1863, aged 70 years; Permelia, his wife, died Feb. 9th, 1840, aged 37 years; Caroline, second wife, died April 23rd, 1872, aged 59 years.

Henrietta, wife of Spencer H. Platt, died March 1st, 1874, aged 39 years.

Andrew Oatman died May 10th, 1835, aged 49 years; Phebe, his wife, died July 8th, 1870, aged 84 years.

Electa Oatman died———, 1835, aged 14 years.

Diana Oatman died May, 1845, aged 36 years.

Safford Oatman died March, 1878, aged 70 years.

Joseph M. Jewett died 1847, aged about 83 years; Phœbe, his wife, died 1843, aged about 73 years; and of their children, Elsie *Huntley* died May 10th, 1832, aged 44 years; Nathan died several years ago in advanced life; Lovisa *Walters* died April 15th, 1823, aged 23 years; Holland died Aug., 1875, aged 70 years; Willard died about 40 years ago in middle life; Hannah, wife of Holland, died Oct. 1878, aged———.

Nathaniel Hubbard came to Wayne in 1809, died Sept. 8th, 1834, aged 60 years; Lucy, his wife, died Nov. 10th, 1848, aged 72 years.

James N. Barber died Oct. 17th, 1860, aged 82 years; Elizabeth, his wife, died Jan. 18th, 1848, aged 68 years; Joseph B. Barber died Aug. 4th, 1856, aged 57 years; Abby Barber died March 28th, 1857, aged 28 years; Billings Barber died Sept. 17th, 1861, aged 34 years; and of the children of Billings and Emily Barber, Abby Barber died Feb. 28th, 1872, aged 15 years; Katie Barber died Jan. 2nd, 1862, aged 10 years.

Norman Wilcox moved from Barkhamsted, Conn., and settled in Wayne in 1817, and died Feb. 16th, 1866, aged 92 years; Rebecca, his wife, died May 10th, 1878, aged 99 years and 11 months; Gamaliel, son of Norman and Rebecca Wilcox, died Feb. 6th, 1851, aged 53 years; Malinda, his wife, died Dec. 12th, 1842, aged 42 years.

Eunice, wife of Norman Wilcox, Jr., died March 4th, 1852, aged 36 years.

Electa, daughter of Norman Wilcox, married Curtis P. Sheldon, and died Oct. 11th, 1879, aged 82 years; Curtis P. Sheldon died April 9th, 1857, aged 68 years.

Walter Walker died April 13th, 1842, aged 83 years; Lois, his wife, died Aug. 21st, 1853, aged 85 years.

Josiah Walker died———1873, aged 87 years; Eunice, his wife, died———1847, aged 55 years.

James Walker died Aug. 23rd, 1851, aged 28 years.

Climena Wilcox died Jan. 24th, 1858, aged 91 years.

Justin Gillett died Aug. 1868, aged 83 years; Armenta, his wife, died Jan. 4th, 1842, aged 53 years.

Wm. R. Gillett died July 26th, 1872, aged 45 years.

Hannah, wife of Lucius Gillett, died Aug. 26th, 1875, aged 53 years.

Mrs. Keen, mother of Mrs. G. W. Dillon, died March 15th, 1878, aged 80 years.

Wm. Campbell died June 11th, 1867, aged 54 years.

Isaac Bradley died March, 1860, aged 92 years.

Dr. L. B. Bradley died Oct. 26th, 1869, aged 65 years; Ursula, his wife, died May 28th, 1873, aged 59 years; Lucelia, daughter of L. B. and Ursula Bradley, died Dec. 24th, 1869, aged 32 years; Hattie, daughter of the same, died Jan. 20th, 1873, aged 28 years.

Reuben Ressell died 1865, aged 68 years; Flizabeth, his wife, died July 12th, 1850, aged 63 years.

Rev. Ephraim T. Woodruff died Nov. 26th, 1859, aged 82 years; Sally, his wife, died 1829.

Rev. Geo. Roberts died May 17th, 1857, aged 50 years.

Chester Fancher died April 2nd, 1857, aged 59 years; Jane, his wife, died March 11th, 1870, aged 76 years.

Archibald Black died Sept., 1868, aged 85 years; his wife died Sept. 1867, aged 84 years.

Sylvester Fitts died Dec. 5th, 1871, aged 82 years; Emily, his wife, died April 10th, 1876.

Sylvanus Cook died Nov. 13th, 1871, aged 72 years.

George Marvin died Sept. 13th, 1873, aged 67 years; Morgan Marvin, son of George Marvin, died May 6th, 1857, aged 24 years.

James W. Foster died March 19th, 1856, aged 83 years; Jane, his wife, died June 20th, 1830, aged 46 years.

Samuel Foster died Oct., 1858.

Erastus S. Foster died March 31st, 1871, aged 56 years.

Wm. Sirrine died June 3rd, 1842, aged 82 years.

Eli Barton died Feb. 9th, 1854, aged 61 years; Marcy, his wife, died April 27th, 1871, aged 80 years.

Lois, wife of Daniel Barton, died April 15th, 1850, aged 81 years.

Henry P. Wilder died March 2nd, 1875, aged 63 years.

Hannah, wife of Thomas Partridge, died March 29th, 1814, aged 31 years.

Austin Holcomb died May 25th, 1864, aged 42 years.

Benjamin Mullett died Aug. 26th, 1875, aged 84 years; Maria, his wife, died Nov. 29th, 1857, aged 57 years; Maria *Flemming*, daughter of Benjamin and Maria Mullett, died June 8th, 1876, aged 38 years.

Wm. S. Mathews died Sept., 1863, aged 61 years.

Sarah, wife of Linus M. Mathews, died Sept., 1853, aged 26 years.

Abram Griffin died Jan 24th, 1879, aged 84 years.

Richard J. Petrie died Feb. 11th, 1849, aged 77 years.

Esther, wife of N. L. Smith, died April 7th, 1863, aged 42 years.

Lyman Leonard died May 9th, 1873, aged 66 years.

Eliphelet Clark died Feb. 23rd, 1854; ———, his wife, died March 16th, 1854, aged 42 years.

Joel Pease, Capt. in the war of 1812, died Oct. 3rd, 1844, aged 84 years; Arsinath, his wife, died Oct. 22nd, 1840, aged 59 years.

Sally, wife of Asa Burns, died June 6th, 1842, aged 54 years.

Francis P. Brown died July 24th, 1864, aged 93 years.

Betsy, wife of Joel Pease, died Sept. 15th, 1875, aged 73 years.

Sevier Niles died Aug. 1st., 1879, aged 79 years.

Susan, wife of Lyman Fields, died April 11th, 1869, aged 73 years.

Joel Kibbce died March 3rd, 1861, aged 74 years.

Deacon Calvin Andrews died Feb. 20th, 1864, aged 73 years; his mother-in-law Mrs. Mary Gates, died Aug. 12th, 1854, aged 97 years.

Temperance Andrews *Follett* died Nov. 23rd, 1875, aged 52 years.

Samuel Andrews died April 13th, 1850, aged 63 years; his second wife, Hulda, died Feb. 18th, 1824, aged 20 years; Lodema, daughter of Samuel, died Feb. 14th, 1854, aged about 20 years; Benoni Andrews died April 27th, 1876, aged 67 years; Edward A., son of Benoni, died Nov. 30th, 1851, aged 18 years.

Charles Walworth died Jan. 13th, 1856, aged 79 years; Miriam, his wife, died Aug. 21st, 1871, aged 92 years.

John Kennedy died Feb. 7th, 1853, aged 56 years; Margaret, his wife, died April 13th, 1849, aged 54 years; James, son of John and Margaret, died May 5th, 1865; Agnes Kennedy died May 15th, 1879, aged 46 years.

David Smilie moved to Wayne in June, 1838, died Jan. 7th, 1871, aged 76 years; Alison, his wife, died June 11th, 1878, aged 81 years.

H. G. Dean died May 23rd, 1864, aged 77 years; Rebecca, his wife, died March 9th, 1873, aged 82 years.

Elihu Allen died Jan. 8th, 1836, aged 72 years; Smith Allen died Dec. 25th, 1842, aged 29 years.

Pauline Cook Dodge died March 15th, 1871, aged 67 years.

Samuel Leonard died Sept. 28th, 1858.

Arthur B. Knowles died Aug. 3d, 1879, aged 59 years.

Among the early settlers in the south part of the town was Edward Inman and Family. Nothing of note regarding the family, except that Stephen committed suicide; another one was caught by the arm in a tree top, while hunting ducks' nests, and hung there for six weary hours before being released; another one had his finger bit off by poking fun at a rattlesnake. They all soon emigrated west.

Having finished the work assigned us, of correcting and republishing the proceedings of the Fiftieth Anniversary of the Settlement of the Township, together with that of the Seventy-Fifth Anniversary, we respectfully submit the same.

PUBLISHING COMMITTEE.